MOVE WITH
CLARITY

The Strategic Destiny Blueprint
to Master Your Wealth, Health, and Relationships

MASTER JUDITH MCKENZIE

Title of the Book: Move With Clarity

Subtitle: The Strategic Destiny Blueprint to Master Your Wealth, Health, and Relationships

Copyright © 2025 by Master Judith McKenzie

All rights reserved. This book or any portion thereof may not be reproduced or used in any manner whatsoever without the express written permission of the author, except for the use of brief quotations in a book review or a scholarly journal.

Published by: East West Feng Shui Solutions

ISBN-979-8-218-78080-7

Disclaimer: A Note on Your Strategic Toolkit

This book is for educational and personal-development purposes only and is not a substitute for professional legal, medical, financial, or psychological advice. The author and publisher assume no liability for any actions taken based on this material.

Case studies are inspired by real consultations but have been altered for privacy: names, professions, and identifying details have been fictionalized. Any resemblance to actual persons is coincidental.

Use of this content is at the reader's own discretion and responsibility.

A Strategic Note on Wealth, Health, and Relationships

On wealth: The financial insights offer a strategic framework for understanding your personal wealth blueprint. They are not a substitute for professional financial planning, legal, or investment advice. Always consult with a licensed professional for specific financial matters.

On health: The health insights presented provide a conceptual framework for understanding the energetic roots of well-being. They are not an alternative for a diagnosis, treatment, or advice from a qualified medical professional. Always consult with a licensed healthcare provider for specific health concerns.

On relationships: The relational insights are designed to help you understand personal tendencies and navigate dynamics with greater awareness. They are not a replacement for professional relationship counseling or therapy.

Use the wisdom in this book to empower your decisions and inspire personal transformation.

For my husband,
Tim,
for your unwavering love and support,
which made this journey possible.

And for my children:

Maria

Shannon

Paola

Jullan

Joeven

You are my greatest joy and
my deepest inspiration.

Contents

Foreword	1
The Blueprint Revealed: My Journey to Clarity	3
Your First Strategic Move: Committing to Your Clarity	5
Your Power Source: Unlocking the Strategic Advantage of Your Blueprint	6
Your Master Key: The Power of BaZi to Unlock Your Source	8
The First Command: Plotting Your Strategic Blueprint	9
Your Tactical Map: Navigating Your Chart for the Clarity	10
The BaZi Destiny Chart	11

Part 1
The Foundation of Your Blueprint — 12

Chapter 1
The Cosmic Trinity – Your Strategic Code for Success — 13

The Cosmic Trinity: A Three-Pillar Framework	13
Heaven Luck: The Luck You Were Born With	14
Earth Luck: The Influence of Your Environment	15
Man Luck: The Power of Your Choice	16
Your Strategic Imperative	17

Chapter 2
The Five Elements – The Foundational Architecture of Your Being — 18

The Wood Element	19
The Fire Element	19
The Earth Element	20
The Metal Element	20
The Water Element	21

Chapter 3
Interplay of the Elements – Cycles of Interaction — 23

Production Cycle: The Cycle of Nurturing and Support	24
Controlling Cycle: The Cycle of Regulation and Balance	25
Weakening Cycle: The Cycle of Draining and Expression	26

Chapter 4
Your Day Master – The Heart of Your Code — 28
The Day Master: Your Personal Point of Power — 28
Sample BaZi Chart: Yang Metal Day Master — 29
Yang Wood: Tree — 30
Yin Wood: Flower — 31
Yang Fire: Sun — 32
Yin Fire: Candle — 33
Yang Earth: Mountain — 34
Yin Earth: Soil — 35
Yang Metal: Blade — 36
Yin Metal: Gem — 37
Yang Water: Ocean — 38
Yin Water: Dew — 39
Your Day Master Is the Ultimate Game-Changer — 40

Part 2
Your Blueprint in Motion — 41
Chapter 5
The Ten Gods – The Architect of Your Influence — 42
Sample BaZi Chart: Direct Resource (DR) Profile — 43
How to Find Your Core Energetic Profile — 44
Animal Signs and Their Main Hidden Element — 45
Resource: Your Learning and Support — 46
Resource Strategic Insight — 46
Companion: Your Peers and Independence — 47
Companion Strategic Insight — 47
Output: Creativity and Expression — 48
Output Strategic Insight — 48
Wealth: Your Finances and Relationships — 49
Wealth Strategic Insight — 49
Influence: Your Career and Authority — 50
Influence Strategic Insight — 50

Chapter 6
Your Core Energetic Profile by Your Month — 52
Direct Resource (DR) Profile — 53
Indirect Resource (IR) Profile — 55
Friend (F) Profile — 57
Rob Wealth (RW) Profile — 59
Eating God (EG) Profile — 61
Hurting Officer (HO) Profile — 63
Direct Wealth (DW) Profile — 65
Indirect Wealth (IW) Profile — 67
Direct Officer (DO) Profile — 69
Seven Killings (7K) Profile — 71

Part 3
The Blueprint for Wealth — 74

Chapter 7
Your Professional Destiny: From Energetic Code to Wealth — 75
Your Professional Compass — 75
Resource: Intellectual Capital — 76
Companion: You Are the Epicenter of Your Enterprise — 78
Output: Innovation and Influence — 80
Wealth: Your Career Is a Legacy of Capital — 82
Influence: Authority and Strategic Control — 84

Chapter 8
The Abundance Matrix: Forging Your Empire of Wealth — 87
I. Industries and Investments by Element — 88
Wood: The Market Pioneer — 88
Fire: The Momentum Catalyst — 90
Earth: The Foundation Fortress — 92
Metal: The Value Arbitrator — 94
Water: The Market Oracle — 96

II. Financial Strategy by Energetic Profile   98
From Talent to Capital: Your Energetic Financial Edge   98
Command Your Capital: Your Energetic Wealth Strategy   98
Direct Resource (DR): The Investment Strategist   99
Indirect Resource (IR): The Market Futurist   100
Friend (F): The Alliance Builder   101
Rob Wealth (RW): The Dealmaker   102
Eating God (EG): The Venture Innovator   103
Hurting Officer (HO): The Paradigm Shifter   104
Direct Wealth (DW): The Capital Manager   105
Indirect Wealth (IW): The High-Leverage Investor   106
Direct Officer: The Corporate Governor   107
Seven Killings (7K): The Crisis Master   108

Chapter 9
Financial Strategy in Action   110
The FEAR That Funds the Stagnation (Investment Avoidance)   111
The RISK That Funds the Collapse (Foundational Neglect)   112
The BETRAYAL That Funds the Loss (Affinity Reliance)   113
The MISCALCULATION That Funds the Failure (Competitive Blindness)   114
The PERFECTION That Funds the Exhaustion (Perfectionism Paralysis)   115
The IMAGE That Funds the Lie (Ego Debt)   116
The CONTROL That Funds the Opportunity Cost (Process Rigidity)   117
The THRILL That Funds the Crash (The Fast Lane Fallacy)   118
The FEAR That Funds the Freeze (Financial Compliance Trap)   119
The INTENSITY That Funds the Chaos (Sudden Financial Eruption)   120

Part 4
The Blueprint for Relationships   122

Chapter 10
The Relational Profiles – Your Energetic Code for Love   123
Direct Resource (DR) Profile: The Resilient Anchor   124
Indirect Resource (IR) Profile: The Intuitive Companion   125
Friend (F) Profile: The Independent Ally   126
Rob Wealth (RW) Profile: The Charismatic Partner   127
Eating God (EG) Profile: The Nurturing Visionary   128
Hurting Officer (HO) Profile: The Discerning Catalyst   129

Direct Wealth (DW) Profile: The Steadfast Provider ... 130
Indirect Wealth (IW) Profile: The Generous Trailblazer ... 131
Direct Officer (DO) Profile: The Principled Balancer ... 132
Seven Killings (7K) Profile: The Relentless Champion ... 133

Chapter 11
Mastering Relational Friction ... 134
Direct Resource (DR) Profile: The Challenge of Detachment ... 135
Indirect Resource (IR) Profile: The Emotional Misfire ... 136
Friend (F) Profile: The Vulnerability Barrier ... 137
Rob Wealth (RW) Profile: The Validation Trap ... 138
Eating God (EG) Profile: The Avoidance of Conflict ... 139
Hurting Officer (HO) Profile: The Critical Analyst ... 140
Direct Wealth (DW) Profile: The Rigidity Trap ... 141
Indirect Wealth (IW) Profile: The Commitment Conundrum ... 142
Direct Officer (DO) Profile: The Unyielding Idealist ... 143
Seven Killings (7K) Profile: The Unrelenting Executor ... 144

Chapter 12
Nurturing Your Connections ... 145
A Strategic Framework for Deeper Bonds ... 145

Chapter 13
The Relational Profiles in Action - Case Studies ... 147
Case Study: Grace ... 148
Case Study: Harry ... 149
Case Study: Luis ... 150
Case Study: Anya ... 151
Case Study: Charlotte ... 152
Case Study: Ethan ... 153
Case Study: Lily ... 154
Case Study: Emily ... 155
Case Study: Diana ... 156
Cultivating a Legacy of Connection ... 157

Part 5
The Blueprint for Health ... 158

Chapter 14
The Elemental Guide to Well-Being ... 159
Wood: Pulse of Growth ... 160
Fire: Force of Transformation ... 162
Earth: Essence of Stability ... 164
Metal: Power of Discipline ... 166
Water: Current of Flow ... 168

Chapter 15
Elemental Well-Being in Action – Case Studies — 170
Case Study: Marcus, Battling Chronic Migraines — 171
Case Study: Finn, Dealing with Exhaustion — 172
Case Study: Jonathan, Struggling with Emotional Imbalance — 173
Case Study: Sarah, Finding a Solution for Insomnia — 174
Case Study: Carlos, Grappling with Chronic Fatigue — 175
Case Study: Claire, Overcoming Overthinking — 176
Case Study: Chad, Facing Respiratory Issues — 177
Case Study: Elvie, Tearing Down Emotional Walls — 178
Case Study: Michael, Overcoming Anxiety — 179
Case Study: Helen, Dealing with Hormonal Imbalance — 180
Commanding Your Well-Being: A New Strategic Framework — 181

Chapter 16
Finding Your Center: A Gentle Guide to Emotional Well-being — 182
A Calm Oasis: Five Simple Acts for Immediate Peace — 183
Direct Resource (DR) Profile — 184
Indirect Resource (IR) Profile — 186
Friend (F) Profile — 188
Rob Wealth (RW) Profile — 190
Eating God (EG) Profile — 192
Hurting Officer (HO) Profile — 194
Direct Wealth (DW) Profile — 196
Indirect Wealth (IW) Profile — 198
Direct Officer (DO) Profile — 200
Seven Killings Profile — 202

Chapter 17
Finding Your Center in Action – Case Studies — 204
Case Study: Arvin, Direct Resource (DR) Profile — 205
Case Study: Olivia, Indirect Resource (IR) Profile — 206
Case Study: Ace, Friend (F) Profile — 207
Case Study: Carla, Rob Wealth (RW) Profile — 208
Case Study: Irish, Eating God (EG) Profile — 209
Case Study: Jessie, Hurting Officer (HO) Profile — 210
Case Study: Chris, Direct Wealth (DW) Profile — 211
Case Study: Jessica, Indirect Wealth (IW) Profile — 212
Case Study: Darren, Direct Officer (DO) Profile — 213
Case Study: Rachel, Seven Killings (7K) Profile — 214

Part 6
Move with Clarity   215

Chapter 18
Your Transformation Awaits: The Ripple Effect of Mastery   216
The Unwavering Command of Self   216
Empowered Decision-Making   217
Proactive Problem-Solving and Optimized Resilience   217
The Ripple Effect: Commanding Your World   218

Chapter 19
Commanding Your Legacy:
The Ultimate Investment in Self   219
Your Personal Strategic Playbook   219
Beyond Personal Mastery: The Strategic Command
of Destiny   220
The Next Phase: The Power of Precision and Strategy   223
The Power of Your Personal Timeline: The BaZi Annual
Retainer Service (Ongoing Collaboration)   224
Your Legacy Awaits: Forge Your Destiny   225

Foreword

When Judith first came to Singapore to learn Chinese metaphysics under my personal mentorship, I immediately recognized her passion and determination. Despite cultural and language barriers, she was relentless in her pursuit of knowledge. She absorbed every detail of the training, diligently taking notes and constantly asking the right questions that revealed her depth of curiosity. That kind of dedication is rare—and it was clear to me even then that she was destined to excel in this field.

Over the years, I have had the privilege of training more than 45,000 students worldwide through the Kevin Foong Feng Shui Academy, equipping them with authentic teachings in BaZi, Classical Feng Shui (San He and San Yuan), and Qi Men Dun Jia. Among them, Judith stood out—not only for her mastery of the technical knowledge, but also for her character, integrity, and natural ability to apply these systems to guide others. It is precisely this combination of skill and values that led me to appoint her as our official representative in the Philippines.

Judith's new book is a powerful milestone, not just for her personal journey but also for the growing global reach of authentic Chinese metaphysics. Through her writing, readers will gain access to the wisdom of BaZi and Feng Shui—knowledge that has helped countless of our clients, including Fortune 500 companies and individuals worldwide, achieve clarity, growth, and success. This book will undoubtedly inspire and empower many to take charge of their destiny.

As someone who has witnessed Judith's growth from student to practitioner, I am proud to endorse her work. Her success is also a reflection of what we stand for at Kevin Foong Consulting Group—education, credibility, and results. With this book, Judith continues our shared mission: to bring the profound art of Chinese metaphysics to more people across cultures, enabling them to transform their lives.

Master Kevin Foong
Kevin Foong Consulting Group
Singapore
www.kevinfoongcg.com

The Blueprint Revealed:
My Journey to Clarity

There was a time I felt like I was rowing hard without a rudder—working, striving, and conquering goals, yet never feeling truly on course. In a constant undercurrent of stress, I said yes to opportunities that didn't align, knowing deep down I was destined for more. I felt a pull toward a purpose I couldn't yet name, a calling that felt both immense and just out of reach.

My turning point was not a new career but the discovery of my Destiny Blueprint. It wasn't about mastering an ancient art; it was about understanding myself. The system revealed my natural strengths, exposed my blind spots, and mapped out my timeline of positive luck cycles. For the first time, I saw my life laid out like a strategic chart, showing me not just where I had been, but where I could go.

One moment stands out. At a critical career crossroads, I was facing two enticing opportunities. On paper, both looked great. But my chart told a deeper truth: one path, though lucrative, would drain my energy, while the other, though more challenging, fit perfectly into an upcoming cycle of good fortune. I chose the second path. That single, data-driven choice set me on the fulfilling, sustainable path I am on today.

For the last fifteen years, I've dedicated myself to mastering this strategic wisdom with the guidance of Bazi Destiny and Feng Shui masters in Malaysia, Hong Kong, the US, and Singapore. I even had the profound honor of training under Master Kevin Foong, which was a pivotal moment in my journey. I've gone on to consult with CEOs, politicians, influencers, business owners, entrepreneurs, everyday people, celebrities, and leaders across the globe, helping them apply this ancient wisdom as a modern tool for strategic empowerment. My purpose has become making Chinese metaphysics a practical tool for everyone, which is why I've shared my insights as a columnist for Sun Star Cebu and in various media platforms.

And that's why this book is called *Move with Clarity: The Strategic Destiny Blueprint to Master Your Wealth, Health, and Relationships*—because true success begins with knowing yourself, understanding your path, and making choices that honor both your ambition and your soul.

Move with Clarity,

Master Judith McKenzie
Founder and Strategic Consultant

Your First Strategic Move: Committing to Your Clarity

You have mastered the external world—the markets, the deals, the metrics. Your drive has built a legacy of wealth and influence, and your ambition is legendary. Yet, in the quiet moments between triumphs, you may have found yourself asking if all the discipline and strategy you've applied to your career is working for your health and relationships.

But perhaps you are in a different place—a place of waiting. Maybe you feel something is missing or out of alignment, looking for fundamental guidance and direction to finally start making good on your life's potential.

If you know you are meant for more but simply don't know where to go or what to start, this book is your essential compass. It provides the initial steps and the personalized map you need to take confident action and break free from the confusion.

What if the greatest competitive advantage you could ever possess was not in the market, but within your personal Destiny Blueprint? A blueprint that, once unlocked, can finally align your actions with your most profound truths.

This book is about that blueprint. It will teach you how to analyze your personal design to reveal a clear, strategic path to mastering the three foundational pillars of your life. This is not about achieving more; it is about learning how to move with precision, purpose, and effortless mastery.

This is your key to finally move with clarity.

Your Power Source: Unlocking the Strategic Advantage of Your Blueprint

Understanding your BaZi Destiny Chart is not just about gaining insight; it's about claiming your personal power and learning to command your life with precision. It's the ultimate framework for strategic self-mastery and continuous optimization.

Self-Discovery

Uncover the blueprint of your core personality, innate power centers, and subtle vulnerabilities. This profound self-awareness dissolves self-judgment, allowing you to operate from a position of authenticity and strength, knowing precisely where to lead and where to delegate.

Empowerment

You will gain the foresight to understand the energetic forces at play during pivotal life cycles. This allows you to navigate challenges not as a victim of circumstance, but as a proactive strategist, armed with the resilience to turn every obstacle into an opportunity for growth.

Informed Decision-Making

Move beyond intuition and execute decisions with tactical precision. By aligning your choices with your energetic flow, you can make better choices in your career, relationships, investments, and health, ensuring every action contributes to your long-term success.

Improved Relationships

Decode the energetic makeup of your loved ones, colleagues, and key relationships. This provides you with a profound level of empathy and understanding, dissolving communication barriers and empowering you to foster harmonious, powerful connections that serve your highest good.

Maximize Opportunities

Your chart reveals the precise timing of your life's energetic seasons. You will learn to identify periods of maximum fortune to launch bold initiatives and seize opportunities with full force. Conversely, you will know when to step back, mitigate risk, and conserve energy for a more powerful reentry.

Personal Growth

Utilize your BaZi as a framework for continuous optimization, refining your character and maximizing your potential. It is the ultimate tool for strategic self-improvement, guiding you to areas where you can truly excel and build lasting wealth.

BaZi is a tactical framework for understanding yourself and your journey, empowering you to create a life that truly resonates with your unique essence. It's a journey from wandering to clarity, from feeling adrift to assuming absolute command of your destiny.

Your Master Key:
The Power of BaZi to Unlock Your Source

What if you could hold a personalized intelligence report on your life? A strategic blueprint that decodes your core competencies, maps your potential vulnerabilities, and reveals the precise timing of your most significant opportunities.

This is the power of a BaZi Destiny Chart.

Originating from an ancient system of energetic intelligence, BaZi, or "Eight Characters," is the master key to understanding your personal operating system. It uses the exact moment of your birth to construct a unique energetic profile—a highly intricate code that reveals the dynamic interplay of the Five Elements (Wood, Fire, Earth, Metal, and Water) that define you.

At its core, a BaZi chart is a profound diagnostic tool. It uncovers not only your innate power centers, but also the subtle imbalances and energetic needs that influence your relationships, wealth, health predispositions, and the ebb and flow of your luck cycles.

By decoding this energetic blueprint, you gain a level of self-awareness that is not merely philosophical but fundamentally strategic. It is the first step toward commanding your destiny with purpose and precision.

The First Command:
Plotting Your Strategic Blueprint

Before we can begin our journey into your personal blueprint, you must first create your chart. Your BaZi Destiny Chart is a cosmic snapshot of the precise moment you took your first breath.

It is the fundamental tool you'll need to understand every chapter that follows.

This section will guide you, step by step, on how to plot your unique chart using a reliable BaZi online calculator. It is a simple and essential process that will give you the key to unlocking the rest of this book's wisdom.

What you'll need:

To plot your chart, you will need three pieces of information from the moment of your birth written on your birth certificate:

- Date of birth - the day, month, and year
- Time of birth - the hour and minute
- Time Zone based on your Place of birth - this is crucial for accounting for different time zones

Your Tactical Map: Navigating Your Chart for the Clarity

Step-by-step instructions

1. **Go to any free online BaZi calculator.**

2. **For the calculator I recommend:**
   Visit eastwestfengshuisolutions.com and click the button labeled "**Plot Your BaZi Chart Here.**"

3. **Create a free profile** when prompted to access the calculator.

4. **Check the chart mode before entering your information.**
   In the upper right-hand corner, you will see a button labeled "**PRO**." Click it to switch the setting to "**Divination**." Once this is selected, you are ready to enter your information.

5. **Enter your birth details.**
   - Select the correct **year, month, day,** and **time** of birth.
   - Note that some calculators use **military (24-hour) time** (e.g., 2:00 PM = 14:00).
   - Choose the **time zone** for your place of birth.
   - Enter your **gender at birth**, which is required for calculating future luck cycles.

6. **Generate your chart.**
   After entering your information, click "**Plot**" to create your BaZi Destiny Chart.

7. **Review and save your chart.**
   Your chart will display your **Four Pillars** (Year, Month, Day, Hour), your **Heavenly Stems, Earthly Branches, Day Master,** and the **Ten Gods**—the foundation of your personal blueprint. Save or print a copy, or take a screenshot and keep it on your phone or computer for easy reference throughout the book.

The BaZi Destiny Chart

10 时 Hour	12 日 Day	1 月 Month	1964 年 Year
辛 Xin Yin Metal [劫财 RW] [金]	庚 Geng Yang Metal [日柱 DM] [金]	乙 Yi Yin Wood [正财 DW] [木]	癸 Gui Yin Water [伤官 HO] [水]
巳 Si Yin Fire Snake [火 蛇]	申 Shen Yang Metal Monkey [金 猴]	丑 Chou Yin Earth Ox [土 牛] [空亡 DE]	卯 Mao Yin Wood Rabbit [木 兔]
庚 Geng +Metal F 比肩 丙 Bing +Fire 7K 七杀 戊 Wu +Earth IR 偏印	戊 Wu +Earth IR 偏印 庚 Geng +Metal F 比肩 壬 Ren +Water EG 食神	辛 Xin -Metal RW 劫财 己 Ji -Earth DR 正印 癸 Gui -Water HO 伤官	乙 Yi -Wood DW 正财

Birth details: January 12, 1964, 10:00 am, female

This is a sample BaZi chart for illustrative purposes only.

Part 1
The Foundation of Your Blueprint

This is a guide to self-discovery and an invitation to a new way of navigating the world with intention. Hidden within your birth data is your personal Destiny Blueprint—a profound strategic code that reveals your innate genius, unique strengths, and the most direct path to your ultimate success.

This is the essential first step to mastering yourself, so you can move with clarity.

Chapter 1
The Cosmic Trinity – Your Strategic Code for Success

As we delve into the intricate world of BaZi, it's essential to grasp a foundational concept that dictates all success and fulfillment in life: the Cosmic Trinity.

This ancient wisdom teaches that your destiny is not a single, fixed path but a dynamic interplay of three powerful forces: Heaven Luck, Earth Luck, and Human Luck. Think of them as the three core pillars supporting and fortifying the architecture of your life.

The Cosmic Trinity: A Three-Pillar Framework

Each pillar of the Cosmic Trinity accounts for approximately 33.33% of your life's outcomes, providing a framework to strategically command your success.

Heaven Luck: The Luck You Were Born With

Making up 33.33% of your total luck, your Heaven Luck—also known as your BaZi or Four Pillars of Destiny—is the luck you inherit at birth. It's your personal cosmic blueprint, etched by the moment you entered the world. This fundamental luck explains why some people glide through life with a natural grace, while others seem to face recurring obstacles.

But understanding your Heaven Luck isn't about accepting a fixed fate. It's about gaining awareness and clarity. When you understand your innate strengths and personal timing, you stop pushing against the tide. You learn when to take bold action, when to pause and gather your resources, and when to simply prepare for what's next.

This knowledge empowers you to work with your destiny, not against it. This is the primary focus of BaZi Destiny Analysis and the core objective of this book.

HEAVEN LUCK
(BAZI ASTROLOGY)

Earth Luck: The Influence of Your Environment

Your environment holds a powerful sway over your life, accounting for 33.33% of your luck. This is your Earth Luck, shaped by Feng Shui, the ancient art and science of "Wind and Water." It is the practice of understanding how Qi—the vital, life-giving energy of the universe—flows around you. Feng (Wind) represents how Qi moves and disperses, and Shui (Water) symbolizes how Qi gathers and is retained.

Feng Shui is a profound study of how natural forms, directional forces, and timing can either nourish and energize your living and working spaces or deplete them. It's about consciously living in an environment that supports your success and well-being. While this book centers on leveraging your Heaven Luck, aligning your home and office spaces through positive energy flow or Feng Shui can amplify your innate blueprint by ensuring you're operating from a position of energetic advantage.

EARTH LUCK
(FENG SHUI)

Part 1 | *Chapter 1 : The Cosmic Trinity – Your Strategic Code for Success*

Man Luck: The Power of Your Choice

Man Luck accounts for the final 33.33% of your destiny. This is your freewill, shaped entirely by your actions, thoughts, and decisions.

You hold the power to change your life—to learn new skills, think differently, and make better choices, regardless of your past.

Your ability to create your own luck is amplified when you align your actions with the insights from your BaZi (Heaven Luck) and the positive energy of your surroundings (Earth Luck).

This is the key to mastering your complete destiny.

Part 1 | *Chapter 1 : The Cosmic Trinity – Your Strategic Code for Success*

Your Strategic Imperative

Understanding the Cosmic Trinity empowers you to adopt a holistic, command-oriented approach to life. It demolishes the illusion of fixed destiny and positions you as the sovereign of your outcomes.

This framework helps you decode your Heaven Luck, revealing the cosmic source code of your innate energetic tendencies. Your Earth Luck is the support from the environment you must align with, and your Man Luck is where you actively shape your legacy through deliberate choices and action.

This book will provide you with the strategic tools to leverage your Heaven Luck, empowering you to make intentional decisions that align with your unique blueprint, ultimately building a life of purpose, mastery, and optimal performance.

Part 1 | *Chapter 2 : The Five Elements – The Foundational Architecture of Your Being*

Chapter 2
The Five Elements – The Foundational Architecture of Your Being

Imagine a grand cosmic ecosystem, a dynamic system where five fundamental energies are in constant, strategic interplay, shaping everything in our universe, including your personal blueprint.

These are the Five Elements: Wood, Fire, Earth, Metal, and Water.

In BaZi, these elements are the very language of your destiny chart. Understanding their characteristics is like decoding the source code of your inner world. Each of us possesses a unique composition and dynamic balance of these elements, which influences your core temperament, strategic decision-making, physical resilience, and inherent drive. Let's explore the essence of each element and their strategic implications:

WOOD  FIRE  EARTH  METAL  WATER

The Wood Element

Imagery: A towering tree reaching for the sky. It represents upward momentum, resilience, and the power to expand.

Associations: The color green, the season of spring, and the direction east.

Core nature: Represents growth, vision, and ambition. It's the energy of new beginnings, strategic planning, and leadership.

Attributes: Confident, visionary, decisive, and highly driven. A strong Wood presence gives you the ability to command and lead others toward a collective goal.

The Fire Element

Imagery: A brilliant flame, giving light and heat. It symbolizes rapid expansion, illumination, and the ability to influence.

Associations: The color red, the season of summer, and the direction south.

Core nature: Represents passion, innovation, and strategic transformation. It's the energy of charisma, clear communication, and influence.

Attributes: Charismatic, persuasive, decisive, and a natural communicator. Fire provides the drive to innovate and transform ideas into reality.

The Earth Element

Imagery: A vast, fertile landscape. It symbolizes nourishment, stability, and the ability to create a foundation for all other elements.

Associations: The color yellow, the changing of seasons, and the center.

Core nature: Represents stability, trust, and wealth preservation. It's the energy of reliability, integrity, and grounded action.

Attributes: Loyal, reliable, practical, and highly methodical. A strong Earth presence gives you the ability to build and sustain long-term value.

The Metal Element

Imagery: A polished sword or a precious gem. It symbolizes precision, clarity, and the ability to cut through complexity.

Associations: The color white, the season of autumn, and the direction west.

Core nature: Represents discipline, precision, and efficiency. It's the energy of structure, integrity, and decisive execution.

Attributes: Disciplined, organized, precise, and highly efficient. Metal provides the clarity and focus needed to cut through complexity and execute a plan flawlessly.

The Water Element

Imagery: The deep ocean or a flowing river. It symbolizes fluidity, deep knowledge, and the ability to find a way around any obstacle.

Associations: The color black, the season of winter, and the direction north.

Core nature: Represents wisdom, adaptability, and strategic flow. It's the energy of communication, introspection, and hidden power.

Attributes: Wise, adaptable, resourceful, and highly intuitive. Water provide the ability to navigate complex situations and find creative solutions.

Part 1 | *Chapter 2 : The Five Elements – The Foundational Architecture of Your Being*

As you read through these descriptions, you might already feel a resonance with one or two elements. This is a beautiful first step in understanding your own unique energetic makeup.

Remember, we all possess a blend of these energies, and it's the interplay between them that paints the vibrant picture of your BaZi chart.

Chapter 3
Interplay of the Elements – Cycles of Interaction

With your chart, we can now begin to see how the Five Elements interact with each other in dynamic cycles. The elements are never static; they are in constant motion, nurturing, challenging, and influencing one another in cycles that shape your personality and your destiny.

In this chapter, we will explore the three main interactions: the Production Cycle, the Controlling Cycle, and the Weakening Cycle.

By understanding these relationships, you will begin to see your life's challenges and blessings not as random events, but as natural flow of energy.

Part 1 | *Chapter 3 : Interplay of the Elements – Cycles of Interaction*

Production Cycle: The Cycle of Nurturing and Support

This cycle represents a harmonious flow where one element creates or supports another. Think of it as a nurturing relationship, where one element gives birth to the next.

Wood feeds Fire: Wood (e.g., trees) is fuel for Fire.

Fire produces Earth: Fire (e.g., ash) creates Earth.

Earth produces Metal: Metal (e.g., minerals) is extracted from Earth.

Metal produces Water: Metal (e.g., condensation on metal) creates Water.

Water feeds Wood: Water (e.g., rain) nourishes Wood.

Part 1 | *Chapter 3 : Interplay of the Elements – Cycles of Interaction*

Controlling Cycle: The Cycle of Regulation and Balance

This cycle represents a relationship where one element controls or overcomes another. It's not necessarily negative; rather, it's about maintaining balance and preventing any one element from becoming too dominant. Think of it as a natural check-and-balance system.

Wood controls Earth: Wood (e.g., tree roots) can break up and penetrate Earth.

Earth controls Water: Earth (e.g., a dam) can contain and channel Water.

Water controls Fire: Water (e.g., extinguishing a flame) can put out Fire.

Fire controls Metal: Fire (e.g., a forge) can melt and shape Metal.

Metal controls Wood: Metal (e.g., an axe) can cut Wood.

Part 1 | *Chapter 3 : Interplay of the Elements – Cycles of Interaction*

Weakening Cycle: The Cycle of Draining and Expression

This cycle is often less talked about but equally important. It describes how one element expends its energy by producing another. It's like giving birth—the mother (the producing element) expends energy to create the child (the produced element).

Wood exhausts Water: Wood absorbs Water to grow.

Fire exhausts Wood: Fire burns Wood to sustain itself.

Earth exhausts Fire: Earth absorbs the warmth and light of Fire.

Metal exhausts Earth: Metal is extracted from Earth, depleting it.

Water exhausts Metal: Water is formed from Metal, dulling it.

Part 1 | *Chapter 3 : Interplay of the Elements – Cycles of Interaction*

Understanding the interplay of these cycles within your own chart provides a powerful form of strategic foresight. You can identify your core strengths to leverage and anticipate potential risks in order to mitigate and architect a clear path for sustainable growth. Your destiny is not something to be endured; it is a blueprint to be executed with Clarity.

You have now acquired the essential insights to go deeper, preparing you to apply these powerful principles to your own personal blueprint.

Chapter 4
Your Day Master – The Heart of Your Code

Your BaZi chart is a strategic plan, your Day Master is the cornerstone. It is the central pillar of your chart, representing your core identity, your inherent self, and how you lead and interact with the world.

Knowing your Day Master is the most crucial step in beginning to understand your personal Destiny Blueprint. It provides the foundational knowledge you need to start making informed, intentional decisions.

The Day Master: Your Personal Point of Power

Your Day Master is the Heavenly Stem of the Day Pillar in your BaZi chart. It represents the energy present in the heavens on the day you were born. It is your essence, your "self" element. For a visual reference, see the sample chart on page 29.

All other elements and interactions in your chart are interpreted in relation to your Day Master.

There are ten Day Masters, each a unique expression of the Five Elements in either their Yang (active, expansive) or Yin (receptive, nurturing) polarity.

Part 1 | *Chapter 4 : Your Day Master – The Heart of Your Code*

Sample BaZi Chart: Yang Metal Day Master

Born on January 12, 1964, at 10:00 am, female

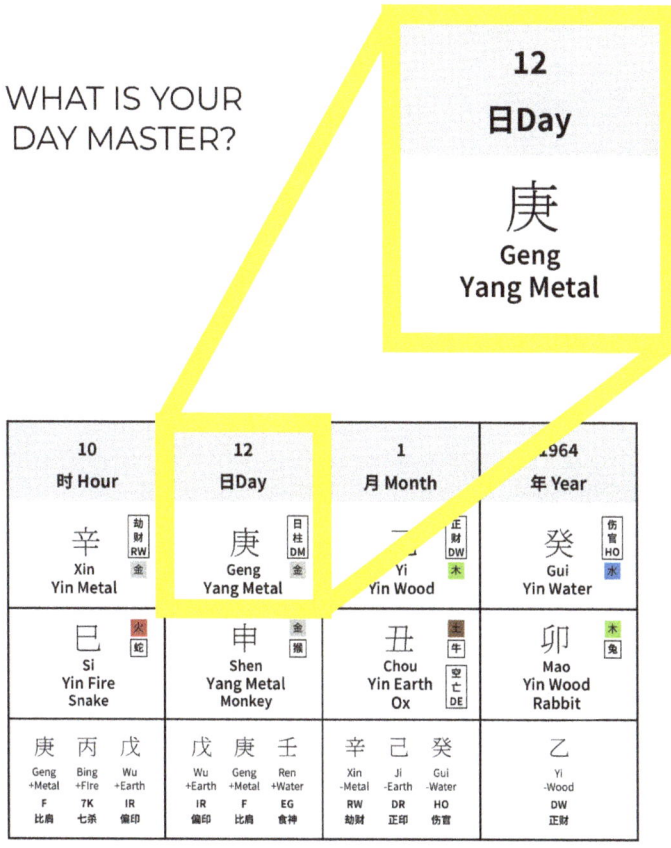

Part 1 | *Chapter 4 : Your Day Master – The Heart of Your Code*

Yang Wood: Tree

Like a towering oak tree, Yang Wood individuals are strong, resilient, and aspire to grow and reach great heights. They are natural leaders, pioneers, and protectors, with a strong sense of justice and desire to make an impact. They can be straightforward, determined, and sometimes a bit inflexible or stubborn. They value independence and have a clear vision.

Understanding your Yang Wood nature helps you embrace your leadership qualities and recognize your need for autonomy and growth. Stand tall in your convictions but remember that even the mightiest tree must bend in the wind to survive so you need to cultivate flexibility.

Artwork by Master Judith McKenzie

Yin Wood: Flower

Like a graceful vine or a beautiful flower, Yin Wood individuals are adaptable, flexible, and charming. They are intuitive, empathetic, and possess a gentle resilience, able to bend without breaking. They are excellent at networking and building relationships, thriving on connection and support. They can be sensitive and sometimes indecisive.

Knowing your Yin Wood essence helps you lean into your adaptability and powerful interpersonal skills. It reminds you of your inherent ability to connect and thrive in various environments, while also encouraging you to strengthen your inner core. Just as a vine needs a trellis, seek out supportive relationships and environments to help you flourish.

Artwork by Master Judith McKenzie

Yang Fire: Sun

Like the radiant sun, Yang Fire individuals are warm, charismatic, and enthusiastic. They are natural entertainers and leaders, bringing light, joy, and optimism wherever they go. They are passionate, direct, and love to be noticed. They can be impatient, impulsive, and sometimes outspoken.

Embracing your Yang Fire nature means harnessing your ability to inspire and illuminate. It encourages you to shine brightly and share your warmth but be mindful that the sun can also scorch. Learn to manage your impulsiveness or the need to always be in the spotlight to avoid burning out or overwhelming others.

Artwork by Master Judith McKenzie

Part 1 | *Chapter 4 : Your Day Master – The Heart of Your Code*

Yin Fire: Candle

Like a flickering candle or distant starlight, Yin Fire individuals are refined, intuitive, and possess a quiet inner warmth. They are highly perceptive, analytical, and insightful, often understanding things on a deeper level. They can be reserved or secretive.

Your Yin Fire essence highlights your deep intuition and analytical mind. It encourages you to trust your inner wisdom and use your subtle influence to guide and illuminate others, while also acknowledging your need for privacy and reflection. You don't need to be the center of attention; your light burns brightest when you're focused on illuminating a path.

Artwork by Master Judith McKenzie

Yang Earth: Mountain

Like a vast mountain, Yang Earth individuals are stable, reliable, and trustworthy. They are grounded, practical, and possess immense patience and resilience. They are natural protectors and providers, offering a sense of security to those around them. They can be stubborn, slow to change, and sometimes overly cautious.

Understanding your Yang Earth nature helps you appreciate your unwavering dependability and be a strong foundation for yourself and others. While stability is your gift, be open to new perspectives and embrace change. A mountain can still have beautiful, flowing rivers.

Artwork by Master Judith McKenzie

Part 1 | *Chapter 4 : Your Day Master – The Heart of Your Code*

Yin Earth: Soil

Like rich, fertile soil, Yin Earth individuals are nurturing, adaptable, and highly supportive. They are empathetic, practical, and excellent at fostering growth in others. They are detail-oriented, diligent, and thrive on creating harmony and stability. They can be prone to worrying, overthinking, and sometimes lack assertiveness.

Your Yin Earth essence speaks to your incredible capacity for nurturing and connecting. Cultivate your supportive nature and create harmonious environments, but remember to nurture yourself as well. Just as soil needs water and nutrients, you need self-care to avoid becoming depleted. Learn to manage your worries and stand up for your own needs.

Artwork by Master Judith McKenzie

Part 1 | *Chapter 4 : Your Day Master – The Heart of Your Code*

Yang Metal: Blade

Like raw iron or a sharp blade, Yang Metal individuals are strong, decisive, and value justice and fairness above all else. They are direct, assertive, and excel at problem-solving and cutting through complexities. They can be blunt, confrontational, and sometimes rigid in their beliefs.

Embracing your Yang Metal nature means recognizing your strength, integrity, and ability to bring about change. It encourages you to stand firm in your convictions and champion what's right. Your decisiveness is a gift, but be mindful of potential harshness. Remember that a blade can be used to build as well as to cut.

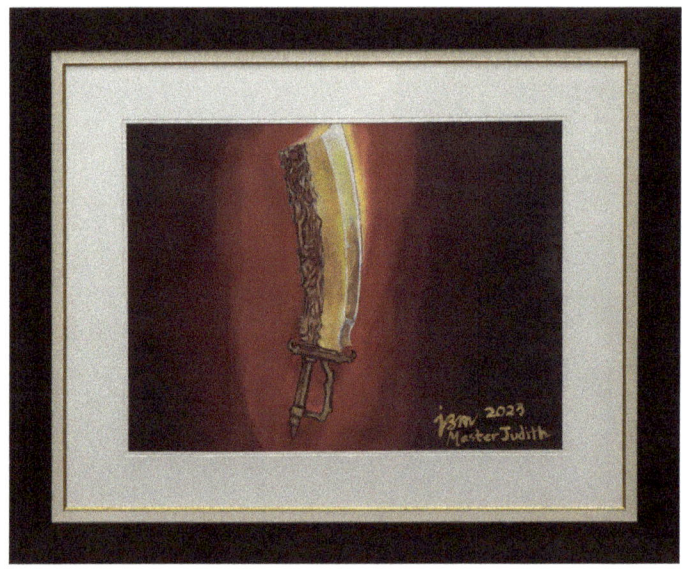

Artwork by Master Judith McKenzie

Part 1 | *Chapter 4 : Your Day Master – The Heart of Your Code*

Yin Metal: Gem

Like a refined jewel or delicate jewelry, Yin Metal individuals are sophisticated, elegant, and highly value beauty and precision. They are discerning, analytical, and possess a keen eye for detail. They strive for perfection and can be self-aware, though sometimes they can be critical, sensitive, or overly concerned with appearances.

Your Yin Metal essence highlights your refined taste and analytical prowess. It encourages you to appreciate beauty and strive for excellence, but learn to manage self-criticism and embrace imperfections. True value comes from your inner brilliance, not just your polished exterior.

Artwork by Master Judith McKenzie

Yang Water: Ocean

Like a boundless ocean or a powerful river, Yang Water individuals are expansive, adaptable, and possess immense wisdom and strategic thinking. They are adventurous and philosophical and thrive on exploration and new experiences. They can be restless, unpredictable, and sometimes prone to overthinking or emotional turbulence.

Understanding your Yang Water nature helps you embrace your adaptability, wisdom, and adventurous spirit. It encourages you to flow with life's currents and explore new horizons. Your wisdom is profound, but be mindful of restlessness or emotional overwhelm. Find ways to calm the waves and connect with your inner depth.

Artwork by Master Judith McKenzie

Yin Water: Dew

Like soft rain, morning dew, or a gentle stream, Yin Water individuals are intuitive, compassionate, and highly adaptable. They are perceptive, reflective, and excellent at understanding human emotions. They thrive on quiet contemplation and can be very supportive, though sometimes they can be secretive, indecisive, or overly sensitive.

Your Yin Water essence speaks to your deep empathy and subtle wisdom. It encourages you to trust your intuition and connect with others on a profound level. Your gentle nature is a source of great strength. Ensure you protect your own energy and avoid becoming overly impressionable.

Artwork by Master Judith McKenzie

Part 1 | *Chapter 4 : Your Day Master – The Heart of Your Code*

Your Day Master Is the Ultimate Game-Changer

Knowing your Day Master isn't just about gaining information—it's about gaining ultimate control over your life's narrative. It's the core engine of your personal blueprint, giving you the strategic insight to:

- **Gain true self-mastery:** Understand who you are at your deepest level and learn to work with your natural flow, not against it.

- **Unleash your strengths:** Move beyond just knowing your talents and start capitalizing on them with laser focus to achieve your goals.

- **Proactively navigate challenges:** Spot potential roadblocks before they appear, turning obstacles into opportunities for growth.

- **Enhance your connections:** Understand your unique energy and how it interacts with others to build stronger professional and personal relationships.

Your Day Master is the essential anchor from which all other insights flow. It's time to stop simply existing and start strategically shaping your destiny with Clarity.

Part 2
Your Blueprint in Motion

You now possess the foundational intelligence of your Destiny Blueprint. But an unapplied insight is a liability. The greatest power lies not in knowing your strategic code, but in putting it into motion.

This part of the book is your command center, in which we translate cosmic principles into a tactical playbook for real-world application.

This is where you will learn to apply your profile to every decision and influence, transforming your understanding into a source of tangible, professional power.

Chapter 5
The Ten Gods – The Architect of Your Influence

If your Day Master is the CEO of your destiny, the Ten Gods represent your executive team—the key operational functions, strategic relationships, and market opportunities that shape your health, career and life. They provide a comprehensive framework for understanding your innate motivations, wealth potential, social dynamics, and areas for strategic growth.

The Ten Gods are derived from the relationship of each of the other Heavenly Stems in your chart to your Day Master, based on the Five Element cycles. They are called "Gods" because they represent archetypal influences and energies—not in a religious sense, but as universal forces that govern your interactions and outcomes. Moving forward, we will call them the Ten Energetic Profiles.

Mastering them is key to unlocking your full potential.

Part 2 | *Chapter 5 : The Ten Gods – The Architect of Your Influence*

Sample BaZi Chart: Direct Resource (DR) Profile

Born on January 12, 1964, at 10:00 am, female

10 时 Hour	12 日 Day	1 月 Month	1964 年 Year
辛 　 劫财 RW Xin Yin Metal 　 金	庚 　 日柱 DM Geng Yang Metal 　 金	乙 　 正财 DW Yi Yin Wood 　 木	癸 　 伤官 HO Gui Yin Water 　 水
巳 　 火 蛇 Si Yin Fire Snake	申 　 金 猴 Shen Yang Metal Monkey	丑 　 土 牛 Chou Yin Earth 空亡 DE Ox	卯 　 木 兔 Mao Yin Wood Rabbit
庚　丙　戊 Geng +Metal　Bing +Fire　Wu +Earth F　7K　IR 比肩　七杀　偏印	戊　庚　壬 Wu +Earth　Geng +Metal　Ren +Water IR　F　EG 偏印　比肩　食神	辛　己　癸 Xin -Metal　Ji　Gui Water RW　DR　 劫财　正印　伤	乙 Yi -Wood DW 正财

**WHAT IS YOUR
ENERGETIC PROFILE?**

DR

43

How to Find Your Core Energetic Profile

Every Animal Sign (or Earthly Branch) in your BaZi chart acts as a container, holding one, two, or even three Hidden elemental energies.

The Energetic Profiles (or Ten Gods) are present in all the hidden elements across the Year Pillar, Month Pillar, Day Pillar and Hour Pillar.

However to determine your Core Energetic Profile with accuracy, we will focus only on the Month Pillar (the pillar that contains the Animal Sign of your birth month).

Check your BaZi Chart and look for the Main Hidden element listed directly below the Animal Sign of the Month you were born.

This Main Hidden Element represents the Principal Qi of the Month Pillar's Earthly Branch, the dominant energy of that pillar, and by identifying this key element, you immediately establish a foundational reference point, your Core Energetic, for your strategic reading.

Part 2 | *Chapter 5 : The Ten Gods – The Architect of Your Influence*

Animal Signs and Their Main Hidden Element

For a quick understanding of your core energetic profile, refer to the table below to find the Main Element of the Animal Sign associated with your birth month. Once you have identified, you can then find its corresponding Energetic Profile, which is located just below the element.

The Animal Sign (also called Earthly Branch)	Month* Based on the Hsia Calendar	The Main Hidden Element (Focus on Birth Month Animal Sign)
Tiger	February	Yang Wood
Rabbit	March	Yin Wood
Dragon	April	Yang Earth
Snake	May	Yang Fire
Horse	June	Yin Fire
Goat	July	Yin Earth
Monkey	August	Yang Metal
Rooster	September	Yin Metal
Dog	October	Yang Earth
Pig	November	Yang Water
Rat	December	Yin Water
Ox	January	Yin Earth

*Key Note: On Timing and Accuracy

The BaZi calendar, also known as the Chinese Solar Calendar or Hsia Calendar, does not follow the Gregorian calendar. The BaZi year officially begins on or around February 4th (known as Lichun or the Start of Spring). Furthermore, the individual months usually begin on either the 5th, 6th or 7th day of the Gregorian month, not the 1st. The exact shift between all Animal Signs is based entirely on the Solar Terms (the Sun's position) for that specific month or year. Therefore, to ensure complete accuracy, you must always use a professional BaZi calculator.

Resource: Your Learning and Support

1. **Direct Resource (DR):** This is your wisdom and formal knowledge. It represents your capacity for structured learning, disciplined study, and receiving guidance from established mentors. This is the nurturing, protective energy that builds a foundation of expertise.

2. **Indirect Resource (IR):** This is your unconventional insight and intuitive genius. It represents your talent for absorbing wisdom from unique sources, solving complex problems creatively, and gaining profound spiritual or philosophical understanding. This is the energy of spontaneous insight and breakthrough solutions.

Resource Strategic Insight

These energies reveal your capacity for learning and your intellectual pursuits, from formal education to intuitive brilliance. They define how you acquire knowledge and receive support, both of which are critical for sustainable growth and a commanding presence. For both male and female charts, these energies also represent the strategic and nurturing dynamics of your relationship with your mother.

Companion: Your Peers and Independence

1. **Friend (F):** This is your sovereign independence and the support you gain from strategic peers and allies. This energy is about a powerful form of self-reliance, giving you the ability to stand on your own while building a network of equals.

2. **Rob Wealth (RW):** This is your relentless competitive spirit and aggressive drive for independence. It's about asserting yourself to claim what's yours and achieving mastery in high-stakes environments. This energy is a potent force for a breakthrough.

Companion Strategic Insight

These energies reveal the architecture of your relationships with peers, your capacity for independence, and your core competitive drive. They illuminate how you build your network and how you navigate the strategic dynamics of collaboration and competition.

Output: Creativity and Expression

1. **Eating God (EG):** This is your natural talent, intuitive creativity, and inner joy. It's about expressing your core essence in a way that is natural, comfortable, and deeply fulfilling, making you a compelling and approachable presence.

2. **Hurting Officer (HO):** This is your raw, powerful intelligence, disruptive innovation, and rebelliousness. It's about expressing yourself in a clever, outspoken, and unconventional style. This energy is a force for change, unafraid to challenge the status quo to achieve a greater vision.

Output Strategic Insight

These energies reveal your capacity for strategic expression, innovation, and how you channel your energy outward to influence others. A strong output indicates a profound drive for freedom and self-expression, which can be leveraged for impactful communication and creative leadership.

Wealth: Your Finances and Relationships

1. **Direct Wealth (DW):** This is your consistent revenue stream, your stable, earned income like a salary. It represents disciplined execution, hard-earned gains, and the accumulation of tangible assets. This is the wealth that comes from your steadfast commitment and focused effort.

2. **Indirect Wealth (IW):** This is your capital-driven wealth and strategic windfall. It represents a capacity for calculated risk-taking, the value of your network, and your ability to leverage opportunities for explosive growth. Think of it as speculative wealth from ventures, investments, or unexpected bonus.

Wealth Strategic Insight

These energies reveal the architecture of your financial destiny, illuminating how you are designed to attract, manage, and grow wealth. They define your financial luck and your relationship with money as a tool for building your legacy. For a male chart, these energies also speak to the strategic and emotional dynamics within your relationship with your spouse.

Influence: Your Career and Authority

1. **Direct Officer (DO):** This is your discipline and unwavering integrity. It represents your capacity for command, reputation, and authority through adherence to a proven system. You are a natural leader who commands respect through fairness and principled action.

2. **Seven Killings (7K):** This is your raw courage and disruptive power under pressure. It represents your ability to overcome adversity and assert unconventional leadership. It's about a relentless, sometimes aggressive, drive to innovate and seize command in the most challenging of environments.

Influence Strategic Insight

These energies are the engines of your career and authority, revealing the architecture of your leadership style and your ability to command respect. They illuminate how you handle pressure and how you are seen by others in positions of power. For a female chart, these energies also speak to the strategic and emotional dynamics within your relationship with your husband.

The true value of the Ten Energetic Profiles lies not in their individual definitions but in their dynamic interplay as the core architecture of your influence.

You can now see your blueprint as a master architect would: identifying where your creative output generates sustainable wealth, where your disciplined resources can strengthen your influence, and how to leverage the competitive spirit of your companion to build powerful alliances.

This knowledge gives you a profound strategic advantage, allowing you to proactively mitigate risks and amplify your strengths with unparalleled precision.

This knowledge transforms you from a passive observer of your chart into the active commander of your destiny. You are no longer navigating the world by chance; you are orchestrating your influence with intent to align with your Destiny Blueprint.

Chapter 6
Your Core Energetic Profile by Your Month

This is where the strategic elements of your BaZi blueprint truly come to life.

While your entire chart is a complex architecture, one of the Energetic Profiles often holds a dominant position, forming what we call your core operational directive.

This singular energetic profile shapes an estimated 70% of your core personality, revealing your innate tendencies and how you instinctively command your world.

By decoding this foundational profile (see image on page 43), you unlock a significant competitive edge. You can consciously leverage your strengths and proactively mitigate your weaknesses with a newfound level of clarity.

Direct Resource (DR) Profile

If your chart is defined by the Direct Resource profile, you are a master of strategic wisdom and foundational strength. You are not a builder; you are an architect. Your power lies in your disciplined pursuit of knowledge and your ability to create unshakable systems. You are the definitive authority.

Traits to Embrace and Maximize

- **Systematic authority:** You have an innate ability to acquire, organize, and distill complex information into a clear, actionable framework.

- **Strategic foresight:** Your deep-rooted wisdom allows you to see beyond the immediate chaos and anticipate future trends and challenges.

- **Unwavering integrity:** You command respect through your reliability, credibility, and principled adherence to a proven process.

- **Quiet power:** Your influence is subtle yet profound, building trust and loyalty through your steadfast, nurturing presence.

Tendencies to Navigate and Manage

- **Overanalysis:** The tendency to gather too much information can lead to analysis paralysis, slowing down your ability to execute.

- **Resistance to change:** Your belief in proven systems can make you rigid and resistant to novel or unconventional ideas, potentially causing you to miss key opportunities.

- **Energy drain:** A focus on giving and nurturing others can lead to neglecting your own needs, resulting in burnout.

Direct Resource (DR) profile strategic growth

- **Focus on execution:** You must learn to trust your wisdom and transition from planning to action. Your knowledge is a tool, not a fortress.

- **Embrace the unconventional:** Actively seek out and explore new, nontraditional ideas. This allows you to expand your powerful framework beyond established norms.

- **Master the exchange:** Learn to balance giving with receiving. Delegate to others to build their authority while freeing yourself to focus on your highest-level work.

By understanding this blueprint, you are now ready to command your domain and move with clarity.

Indirect Resource (IR) Profile

If your chart is defined by the Indirect Resource profile, you are a master of unconventional wisdom and intuitive genius. You don't follow the map; you create it. Your power lies in your ability to connect disparate ideas and solve complex problems in a way no one else can. You are a source of breakthrough solutions.

Traits to Embrace and Maximize

- **Unconventional insights:** You have a profound ability to see the world differently, allowing you to discover new opportunities and solutions that others miss.

- **Intuitive genius:** Your gut instinct is a powerful strategic tool. You can absorb information and understand situations without needing a logical process.

- **Creative problem-solving:** Your mind is a creative engine, capable of generating novel and often disruptive solutions to long-standing challenges.

- **Strategic independence:** You thrive when you have the freedom to think and work without being constrained by rigid systems or traditional authority.

Tendencies to Navigate and Manage

- **Lack of focus:** Your mind's constant flow of ideas can lead to a lack of focus, making it difficult to complete projects and bring ideas to fruition.

- **Resistance to systems:** Your natural rebellion against the norm can cause you to dismiss valuable, established systems and structures, which can hinder your own progress.

- **Unrealistic ideation:** Your groundbreaking ideas may lack practicality, becoming too ungrounded to be executed effectively.

Indirect Resource (IR) Strategic Growth

- **Master the discipline of action:** Learn to ground your brilliant ideas by partnering with those who can help you execute and build a clear path to market.

- **Create your own system:** Instead of rejecting all systems, learn to build your own. This will help you channel your creativity into a scalable and repeatable process.

- **Channel your genius:** Identify your most powerful insights and focus your energy on them. Your genius is a resource to be managed, not a free-flowing river.

By understanding this blueprint, you move beyond brilliant ideas to become the unstoppable force of innovation the world has been waiting for—empowered to move with clarity.

Friend (F) Profile

If your chart is defined by the Friend profile, you are a master of sovereign independence and powerful alliances. You are not defined by others; you are your own authority. Your power lies in your ability to stand on your own two feet while building a strategic network of equals who respect your self-reliance.

Traits to Embrace and Maximize

- **Unwavering self-reliance:** You possess a powerful and innate sense of independence, making you a definitive source of your own strength and security.

- **Strategic alliances:** Your ability to relate to peers as equals allows you to build a powerful and mutually beneficial network based on trust and shared values.

- **Powerful sovereignty:** You are your own commander, unafraid to make decisions and take action based on your own counsel and inner wisdom.

- **Clear judgment:** You are less swayed by external pressures and emotional influence, allowing you to make clear, objective decisions.

Tendencies to Navigate and Manage

- **Excessive independence:** Your self-reliance can lead to a reluctance to ask for help, even when a team effort would lead to a far more effective outcome.

- **Relational detachment:** Your focus on independence can sometimes cause you to be emotionally distant from others, hindering deep connection.

- **Inability to collaborate:** You may struggle to operate within a traditional team structure, preferring to lead or work alone, which can limit your scale.

Friend (F) Profile Strategic Growth

- **Master the art of collaboration:** Understand that your independence is an asset, but true power lies in a strategic network. Learn to delegate and trust your peers to multiply your effectiveness.
- **Cultivate your network:** Don't just rely on your own strength. Actively and intentionally build your inner circle and your strategic allies.
- **Leverage your solitude:** Your best ideas often come from quiet introspection. Structure your time to get the most from your moments of independent thought before you execute with a team.

Rob Wealth (RW) Profile

If your chart is defined by the Rob Wealth profile, you are a master of relentless competitive drive and aggressive independence. You are not just a player; you are a force of nature. Your power lies in your fierce will to win and your unshakable conviction that you can overcome any obstacle to secure your destiny.

Traits to Embrace and Maximize

- **Relentless competitive drive:** You are wired to compete and win. This innate drive is a powerful engine for achieving your goals and outperforming everyone in your field.

- **Aggressive independence:** You possess a profound desire to stand on your own two feet and seize control. You are not afraid to challenge the status quo to build your own empire.

- **Mastery in competition:** You thrive in high-stakes, competitive environments. Your ability to think on your feet and make decisive moves gives you a powerful advantage.

- **Strategic assertiveness:** You are not afraid to be direct, negotiate hard, and assert your will, making you a formidable force in business and life.

Tendencies to Navigate and Manage

- **Overly competitive:** Your drive to win can lead you to create conflict where none is needed, potentially burning strategic bridges and alienating allies.

- **Risk of financial friction:** Your competitive nature can create a tendency for financial challenges or disagreements, especially with peers or partners.

- **Unnecessary conflict:** You may be so focused on being right and winning that you lose sight of the bigger, more important strategic objective.

Rob Wealth (RW) Profile Strategic Growth

- **Channel your energy:** Focus your competitive energy on a definitive mission and not on trivial battles. Your power is maximized when it's directed toward a purpose bigger than just winning.

- **Build a board of allies:** Learn to see your peers not as rivals but as potential partners. The greatest power is found in a strategic alliance where you can leverage collective strength.

- **Master the art of collaboration:** Learn when to assert yourself and when to work with others. Your drive and their support create an unstoppable force.

Eating God (EG) Profile

If your chart is defined by the Eating God profile, you are a master of creativity and natural talent. Your power lies in your ability to generate compelling ideas and express your inner essence in a way that is natural and deeply fulfilling. You are a source of profound imagination and authentic influence.

Traits to Embrace and Maximize

- **Compelling presence:** Your innate talent gives you a powerful and authentic presence that draws others in.

- **Natural talent:** You have a natural gift for expression, which makes it easy to excel in creative pursuits and strategic communication.

- **Intuitive creativity:** Your best ideas come from a place of flow and intuition, allowing you to generate insights without forcing a process.

- **Strategic comfort:** You thrive by building an environment where you can be yourself, and this authenticity becomes your greatest asset.

Tendencies to Navigate and Manage

- **Lack of discipline:** Your love for ingenuity can lead to a lack of structure, making it difficult to execute projects from start to finish.

- **Subtle procrastination:** The tendency to wait for the "perfect moment" or "perfect feeling" can lead to missed deadlines and lost opportunities.

- **Risk aversion:** Your desire for comfort and ease can make you shy away from the difficult, high-stakes decisions required for major growth.

Part 2 | *Chapter 6 : Your Core Energetic Profile by Your Month*

Eating God (EG) Profile Strategic Growth

- **Monetize your flow:** Learn to build a business model around your natural talents. Your expression isn't just a hobby; it's a strategic revenue stream.

- **Partner for execution:** Align yourself with a more disciplined partner who can help you transform your brilliant ideas into a tangible, scalable reality.

- **Build your platform:** Your ideas deserve to be shared. Create a structured system that consistently delivers your creative output to your audience without waiting for inspiration.

Hurting Officer (HO) Profile

If your chart is defined by the Hurting Officer profile, you are a master of raw intelligence and disruptive innovation. You don't just think outside the box—you incinerate the box. Your power lies in your fearless intellect and your relentless drive to challenge the status quo to achieve a greater vision. You are an unstoppable force for change.

Traits to Embrace and Maximize

- **Unconventional intellect:** Your mind is wired to see a better way. You can instantly spot inefficiencies and devise groundbreaking solutions that bypass traditional methods.

- **Fearless self-expression:** You have an innate ability to speak your truth, challenge authority, and command attention with your clever and outspoken style.

- **Disruptive innovation:** You are a natural innovator who thrives on creating new systems, technologies, and ideas that can redefine an industry.

- **Competitive drive:** Your intense need to prove yourself is a powerful engine for a relentless pursuit of excellence and mastery.

Tendencies to Navigate and Manage

- **Unnecessary rebellion:** Your powerful need to be different can lead to rebelling for the sake of it, creating conflict where none is needed.

- **Lack of collaboration:** Your belief that you know best can make you arrogant, pushing away valuable team members who could help you execute your vision.

- **Unfiltered communication:** Your straightforward nature can be perceived as tactless or aggressive, potentially burning strategic bridges.

Hurting Officer (HO) Profile Strategic Growth

- **Channel your disruption:** Focus your rebellious energy on a specific mission. Don't be a rebel without a cause; be a revolutionary with a plan.

- **Build a strategic team:** Your brilliance is maximized when it is supported by a disciplined and stable team. Learn to trust and delegate to those who can execute your vision.

- **Master the art of influence:** Your ideas will get you noticed, but your ability to communicate them effectively will get you to the top. Learn to package your genius in a way that inspires, rather than offends.

Direct Wealth (DW) Profile

If your chart is defined by the Direct Wealth profile, you are a master of disciplined execution and tangible asset accumulation. You are not a speculator; you are a builder. Your power lies in your unwavering consistency and ability to turn steadfast effort into a secure, predictable revenue stream. You are the definitive commander of your financial domain.

Traits to Embrace and Maximize

- **Disciplined execution:** Your innate ability to follow a plan and execute with precision ensures that every effort yields a tangible result.
- **Strategic stability:** You provide a reliable and consistent force in any team or business, creating a foundation of trust that others can depend on.
- **Unwavering loyalty:** Your dedication to your work, your team, and your assets makes you a powerful partner and an essential leader.
- **Asset accumulation:** You have a natural talent for acquiring and protecting tangible assets, building a legacy of security and wealth.

Tendencies to Navigate and Manage

- **Risk aversion:** Your love for stability can make you hesitant to take the calculated risks necessary for explosive growth and market disruption.
- **Over reliance on tradition:** Your belief in proven methods can make you rigid and slow to adapt to new, innovative opportunities.
- **Limited vision:** You may focus intently on the details of execution that you miss the bigger picture or fail to see a game-changing opportunity.

Direct Wealth (DW) Profile Strategic Growth

- **Embrace calculated risk:** Learn to identify and take on a small degree of risk. Partner with an innovator who can provide the vision while you ensure its disciplined execution.

- **Diversify your blueprint:** Expand your focus beyond traditional, consistent income streams. Leverage your stability to explore new ventures and secure a competitive advantage.

- **Delegate execution:** To free up your time for higher-level strategy, learn to delegate routine tasks to a trusted team.

Indirect Wealth (IW) Profile

If your chart is defined by the Indirect Wealth profile, you are a master of strategic windfall and capital-driven growth. You don't build slowly—you acquire and leverage. Your power lies in your sharp instincts for opportunity and your ability to turn risk into explosive gain. You are a natural disruptor and an aggressive wealth architect.

Traits to Embrace and Maximize

- **Strategic opportunism:** You have a profound ability to spot high-reward opportunities and execute a plan to capitalize on them before anyone else.

- **High-leverage network:** Your social connections and charisma are not a hobby—they are a core strategic asset that you leverage for financial gain and influence.

- **Explosive growth:** You are wired to generate wealth in nontraditional, often speculative ways, making you a force for exponential, rather than linear, growth.

- **Calculated risk-taking:** Your comfort with risk allows you to make decisive moves that others would shy away from, giving you a competitive edge.

Tendencies to Navigate and Manage

- **Lack of foundation:** Your focus on quick gains can cause you to neglect the slow, methodical work of building a stable foundation, leading to instability.

- **Inconsistency:** The pursuit of the next big opportunity can lead to inconsistency in your efforts and an inability to see long-term projects through to the end.

- **Emotional detachment:** Your focus on cold, hard metrics can sometimes lead you to neglect the human element in your relationships.

Indirect Wealth (IW) Profile Strategic Growth

- **Build your base:** Partner with a Direct Wealth individual who can help you ground your ventures and build a stable, consistent foundation beneath your explosive growth.

- **Cultivate patience:** Not every opportunity is a winner. Learn to be patient and discerning with your investments, rather than pursuing every single lead.

- **Command your network:** Consciously cultivate your relationships. Recognize that your influence is your greatest asset, and it is built on mutual trust and respect, not just transactions.

Direct Officer (DO) Profile

If your chart is defined by the Direct Officer profile, you are a master of strategic discipline and unwavering integrity. You are not just a leader; you are a commander. Your power lies in your disciplined adherence to a proven system, your unshakable integrity, and your capacity to command respect through principled action.

Traits to Embrace and Maximize

- **Strategic discipline:** You have an innate ability to create and follow a plan with precision, ensuring consistent and reliable results in any high-stakes environment.

- **Unwavering integrity:** Your powerful sense of responsibility and ethics makes you a source of unshakable trust and a beacon of authority for your team and your network.

- **Principled leadership:** You lead by example, commanding not through force, but through your dignified and consistent application of proven methods.

- **Command authority:** You are a natural authority figure, capable of organizing chaos and leading a team with a clear, calm sense of purpose.

Tendencies to Navigate and Manage

- **Excessive rigidity:** Your respect for rules and structure can make you inflexible and resistant to unconventional methods, potentially causing you to miss key opportunities.

- **Over reliance on the system:** The comfort of a structured system can lead to an inability to adapt when the rules of the game change.

- **Risk aversion:** Your desire for stability and control can make you hesitant to take the aggressive, high-risk actions needed for disruptive innovation.

Direct Officer (DO) Profile Strategic Growth

- **Cultivate flexibility:** Actively seek out new ideas and methodologies. Learn to discern when to break a rule for a greater strategic advantage.

- **Delegate and trust:** To avoid micromanaging, learn to delegate authority and trust your team. Your true power is in leading, not doing.

- **Embrace disruption:** Find a partner or mentor who can provide the vision for radical change, while you provide the strategic discipline to execute it flawlessly.

Seven Killings (7K) Profile

If your chart is defined by the Seven Killings profile, you are a master of unconventional leadership and relentless drive. You are not a follower; you are a force of nature. Your power lies in your raw courage to confront challenges head-on and your ability to innovate under pressure. You are a natural innovator and a powerful agent of change.

Traits to Embrace and Maximize

- **Relentless drive:** You have an intense, unwavering desire to overcome obstacles and achieve your goals, making you unstoppable in the face of adversity.

- **Dynamic leadership:** You thrive in crisis, commanding respect by demonstrating a cool, decisive demeanor when others are overwhelmed.

- **Radical innovation:** Your mind is wired to see a path where others see a dead end. You are a master of finding unconventional solutions and forging new paths.

- **Fearless execution:** Your courage gives you the ability to take on high-stakes, high-pressure challenges and execute a plan with precision and authority.

Tendencies to Navigate and Manage

- **Excessive aggression:** Your relentless nature can be perceived as aggressive or confrontational, potentially creating unnecessary conflict.

- **Risk addiction:** The thrill of a challenge can lead you to take on risks that are not strategically sound.

- **Lack of patience:** Your desire to act quickly can cause you to rush a plan and neglect the critical details needed for long-term success.

Seven Killings (7K) Profile Strategic Growth

- **Channel your power:** Focus your aggressive energy on a single, meaningful mission. Be a revolutionary with a purpose.

- **Build a team of disciplinarians:** To avoid impulsive action, partner with a more stable, grounded individual who can help you refine and execute your vision with precision.

- **Master self-control:** Learn to manage your intense energy. Your power is maximized when it is applied with intentionality, not just passion.

Part 2 | *Chapter 6 : Your Core Energetic Profile by Your Month*

Having uncovered your core energetic profile, you now possess a foundational understanding of the energetic forces that shape your life. This is not just theory, it is the strategic bedrock of your Destiny Blueprint.

By applying this knowledge, you are empowered to reveal your most direct path, unlock your truest potential, and move with clarity from this moment forward.

Part 3
The Blueprint for Wealth

Your professional life is not a ladder to climb; it is a legacy to build. In a world where most people simply drift through their careers, you will learn to move with clarity and create a legacy of wealth and purpose.

This section is your playbook for converting your personal Destiny Blueprint into tangible professional power and financial success.

This is where you move from understanding yourself to intentionally designing your future.

Chapter 7
Your Professional Destiny: From Energetic Code to Wealth

The time for analysis is over. You've decoded your inner architecture and mastered the strategic application of your energetic code. Now, it's time to apply that invaluable data to your professional life—the ultimate proving ground for your power.

This isn't about finding a job; it's about constructing a legacy and building an empire. Your BaZi blueprint is a high-powered strategic tool for identifying a professional path where you operate with uncommon ease and make your most significant contribution to the world. Your career is the ultimate vehicle for your impact, a strategic extension of your deepest self.

By matching your innate energetic code with the nature of a profession, you can master your trajectory and build a career that is not only successful but fundamentally purposeful and aligned with your legacy.

Your Professional Compass

Your Month Pillar is the most potent indicator of your professional path—a granular view of your core approach to work and the talents you can monetize with the greatest efficiency. This is your career's primary data point.

The Energetic Profile in this pillar reveals the strategic roadmap to a profession where you operate with a natural and unique advantage, effortlessly converting your inner code into professional capital.

Resource: Intellectual Capital

Your career is built on the power of your mind. You build your professional empire not with hands-on labor but with the intellectual capital you command.

Direct Resource Profile: The Foundational Strategist

Your professional capital is your expertise. You are a master of systems, excelling in roles that demand meticulous research, disciplined strategy, and an unwavering grasp of theory. You build a legacy by providing the bedrock of knowledge upon which an entire organization can thrive.

Traits: Supportive, nurturing, and knowledge driven

Ideal Professions and Industries

- **Corporate:** Chief research officer, head of research and development (R&D), expert consultant
- **Education and arts:** University provost, education and training, publishing and writing, art and cultural preservation
- **Community-based:** Social work and nonprofits, religious or spiritual services, healthcare (doctors, nurses, holistic practitioners)

Indirect Resource (IR) Profile: The Intuitive Luminary

Your professional capital is your intuition. You are an unconventional visionary, pioneering new fields and solving complex problems with groundbreaking insight. Your mind operates on a different frequency, giving you a predictive edge to navigate uncertainty and discover opportunities others miss.

Traits: Creative, intuitive, and unconventional

Ideal Professions and Industries

- **Technology and innovation:** Artificial intelligence (AI)/data scientist, strategic forecaster, disruptive inventor, R&D
- **Creative industries:** Thought leader, writing, poetry, storytelling, art, music, film
- **Wellness:** Alternative medicine and therapy
- **Entrepreneurial:** Freelancing and consulting

Companion: You Are the Epicenter of Your Enterprise

You are the epicenter of your enterprise. Your career path is defined by your ability to lead, influence, and build powerful coalitions in the pursuit of a shared objective.

Friend (F) Profile: The Alliance Strategist

Your professional capital is your willpower. You are a natural catalyst who forges powerful organizations through fierce loyalty and hands-on leadership.

You build your legacy not alone, but by unifying your team into a cohesive and powerful force.

Traits: Collaborative, competitive, and self-reliant

Ideal Professions and Industries

- **Leadership:** Founder, CEO, corporate strategist, head of business development
- **Entrepreneurship:** Small business ownership, entrepreneurship with a hands-on approach
- **Partnerships:** Partnerships and team-based ventures, shared-economy platforms
- **Community:** Sports and competitive industries, nonprofit groups and community-building initiatives

Rob Wealth (RW) Profile: The Dynamic Leader

Your professional capital is your influence. You are a master networker and dealmaker, leveraging social capital and strategic partnerships to seize market share.

You excel at taking calculated risks and turning competitive tension into professional and financial gain.

Traits: Bold, resource-sharing, and risk-taking

Ideal Professions and Industries

- **Entrepreneurship:** High-risk ventures and startups, entrepreneurship with a hands-on approach
- **Finance and consulting:** Financial consulting or wealth redistribution, real estate flipping or high-volume trading
- **Leadership:** Politician, high-stakes sales executive, financial advisor
- **Technology and community:** Technology platforms for sharing resources, crowdfunding and community-based businesses, partnerships in speculative ventures

Output: Innovation and Influence

You do not just work; you create. Your career path is defined by your capacity to innovate, influence, and leave your own signature on the world.

Eating God (EG) Profile: The Visionary Creator

Your professional capital is your vision. You lead through inspiration, naturally becoming the creative architect of an enterprise. Your greatest strength is your ability to bring a new, original vision to life and define an industry with your unique brand of artistry.

Traits: Creative, expressive, and leisure oriented

Ideal Professions and Industries

- **Creative leadership:** Visionary founder, chief creative officer, master storyteller

- **Arts and entertainment:** Entertainment and performing arts, fashion design and luxury goods

- **Lifestyle:** Culinary arts and gastronomy, wellness and fitness (yoga, lifestyle coaching), travel and leisure industries, children's education, and entertainment

Hurting Officer (HO) Profile: The Disruptive Innovator

Your professional capital is your intellectual disruption. You thrive on challenging the status quo and executing groundbreaking ideas that others would deem impossible.

Your profession is a force of transformation, a catalyst for change that redefines established industries.

Traits: Outspoken, inventive, and competitive

Ideal Professions and Industries

- **Innovation and technology:** Chief technology officer, R&D head, entrepreneurship in innovative sectors, technology, and app development
- **Consulting and strategy:** Maverick consultant, sales and marketing
- **Creative and communication:** Media and broadcasting, public relations and communications, performing arts (actors, musicians, influencers)

Wealth: Your Career Is a Legacy of Capital

You build an empire of assets and returns. Your career path is fundamentally designed for the generation and management of capital, allowing you to build your legacy with strategic financial power.

Direct Wealth (DW) Profile: The Financial Pillar

Your professional capital is your integrity. You excel in a career built on a foundation of meticulous administration, consistent returns, and disciplined growth.

You are the rock of any organization, the one who ensures every asset is accounted for and every return is earned with principled precision.

Traits: Practical, disciplined, and focused on tangible results

Ideal Professions and Industries

- **Finance and administration:** CFO, asset manager, corporate controller, financial planner, accounting and bookkeeping, insurance, and risk management
- **Commerce:** Retail and trading businesses, supply chain and logistics
- **Tangible assets:** Real estate and property investment, agriculture and farming

Indirect Wealth (IW) Profile: The Capitalist Strategist

Your professional capital is your network. You are the visionary dealmaker, thriving in high-leverage ventures and capitalizing on opportunities others miss.

Your greatest skill is in leveraging intangible assets—connections, timing, and insights—to create outsized financial returns.

Traits: Opportunistic, entrepreneurial, and resourceful

Ideal Professions and Industries

- **Finance and investment:** Venture capitalist, investment banker, investments and stock trading, gambling, and speculative ventures

- **Entrepreneurship:** M&A specialist, entrepreneur, marketing and advertising

- **Global commerce:** Import-export and international trade, hospitality and tourism, entertainment, and event management

Influence: Authority and Strategic Control

Your career path is defined by your mastery of authority, discipline, and strategic control. You are a natural leader who commands respect and builds a legacy through systems and influence.

Direct Officer (DO) Profile: The Corporate Pillar

Your professional capital is your authority. You command respect through principled leadership and build a legacy within established institutions.

Your ideal profession is one where you are the master of structure, bringing order and discipline to complex organizations and ensuring long-term stability.

Traits: Responsible, authoritative, and structured

Ideal Professions and Industries

- **Corporate leadership:** CEO, corporate director, corporate management, and leadership
- **Government and law:** Head of governance, senior government official, government and public administration, law and legal consultancy
- **Institutional management:** Education and academia, healthcare and medical administration, regulatory and compliance roles

Seven Killings (7K) Profile: The Strategic Executor

Your professional capital is your courage. You rise through decisive action, thriving in high-pressure turnarounds and commanding difficult missions.

Your strength is in your ability to confront chaos, make the hard choices, and execute with ruthless precision to secure a definitive victory.

Traits: Bold, dynamic, and willing to take risks

Ideal Professions and Industries

- **Leadership and command:** Military general, chief of operations, corporate turnaround specialist, leadership in high-pressure environments
- **Law and security:** High-stakes litigator, law enforcement and security services
- **Crisis and risk:** Emergency services and crisis management, high-risk investments
- **Physical and competitive:** Sports and physical training

Part 3 | *Chapter 7 : Your Professional Destiny: From Energetic Code to Wealth*

Crafting your career masterplan is the ultimate power move. It's the difference between navigating your professional life by chance and directing it with ruthless precision.

You now possess the core data to align your ambition with your innate energies, allowing you to operate in your zone of genius. Your legacy isn't something you hope for; it's something you build.

It's time to leverage your masterplan and proactively shape the future you were born to create.

Chapter 8
The Abundance Matrix: Forging Your Empire of Wealth

Your personal chart is not merely a guide for your career; it is the ultimate roadmap to your financial mastery.

Your chart reveals which industries and investment vehicles are in perfect resonance with your natural energies, making it possible to achieve massive success by design, not by chance.

This chapter is your definitive guide to transforming your unique energetic profile into a powerful, executable financial plan.

Part 3 | *Chapter 8 : The Abundance Matrix: Forging Your Empire of Wealth*

I. Industries and Investments by Element

The Elemental Framework for Financial Command

Your first step toward financial governance is to align your core energetic code with the economic landscape.

By strategically positioning yourself in industries that are in direct congruence with your blueprint, you create a powerful synergy that eliminates friction and unlocks exponential value.

Wood: The Market Pioneer

Wood energy is the blueprint for a commanding, pioneering force in the economic landscape.

It is not just about growth; its core function is to strategically identify new frontiers and lay the foundation for a financial empire where none existed before.

This energy is the architect of the future, forging new value by design.

Core Energy

Wood is the force of expansion, innovation, and leadership. It is the pioneering force that drives new beginnings and cultivates growth.

Strategic Industries and Investment Vehicles

Industries aligned with Wood leverage its core energy for new development and expansion. Think greentech (sustainable energy, carbon credits), education, biotechnology, fashion, and publishing.

Any industry that pioneers new ideas or cultivates talent is in perfect alignment. Portfolios aligned with Wood deploy funds into venture capital, startups, and high-growth stocks within these sectors.

This energy is best suited for early-stage investments that require patient nurturing to mature and create exponential value.

Part 3 | *Chapter 8 : The Abundance Matrix: Forging Your Empire of Wealth*

Yang Wood

Wealth Traits: Resilience, long-term growth, and reliability

Industries

- Real estate development
- Agriculture and forestry
- Construction and infrastructure
- Education and mentorship
- Architecture and urban planning

Yin Wood

Wealth Traits: Creativity, adaptability, and networking

Industries

- Design (interior, fashion, graphic)
- Marketing and advertising
- Public relations and communications
- Entrepreneurship in innovative fields
- Wellness and holistic health

Fire: The Momentum Catalyst

Fire energy's financial command lies in its ability to generate rapid acceleration and seize public momentum.

This is the blueprint of a strategic force that understands speed and visibility are the ultimate leverage.

Fire is an expert at transforming an idea into a dominant force in the market.

Core Energy

Fire energy is the force of transformation, speed, and visibility. It represents innovation, technology, and branding. It's the energy that brings a vision to the world.

Strategic Industries and Investment Vehicles

Industries aligned with Fire synergize with its highly dynamic and cutting-edge nature. This includes fintech, AI, digital media, entertainment, blockchain technology, and aerospace.

This energy thrives in environments where ideas are monetized and scaled rapidly. Portfolios accelerate returns by investing in initial public offerings (IPOs), high-beta stocks, and cryptocurrencies.

This energy excels in fast-moving, high-yield assets.

Yang Fire

Wealth Traits: Visibility, leadership, and influence

Industries

- Media and entertainment (acting, broadcasting)
- Marketing and public speaking
- Event management and promotions
- Renewable energy and technology
- Tourism and hospitality

Yin Fire

Wealth Traits: Strategic thinking, precision, and focus

Industries

- Technology (software development, data analysis)
- Consulting (business or technical)
- Healthcare (specialized practices, medical research)
- Education (focused on advanced or niche skills)
- Arts (film production, photography)

Earth: The Foundation Fortress

Earth energy builds a financial blueprint for unshakable stability and generational wealth.

While others chase volatile gains, its true power is in the strategic art of capital preservation.

It is the ultimate guardian, building an economic fortress that protects assets against any market storm.

Core Energy

Earth energy is the foundation of stability, trust, and wealth preservation. It represents real estate, agriculture, and resource management.

Strategic Industries and Investment Vehicles

Sectors that are stable and foundational to society position themselves by aligning with Earth energy. This includes real estate development, asset management, insurance, agriculture, and hospitality.

This energy is best deployed in ventures that create tangible, lasting value. Legacies are built by focusing on fixed income assets, real estate investment trusts (REITs), land holdings, and blue-chip stocks.

This energy excels at long-term capital preservation and generational wealth creation.

Yang Earth

Wealth Traits: Stability, reliability, and strong foundation building

Industries

- Real estate (property investment, land development)
- Mining and resource extraction
- Infrastructure and public works
- Finance (banking, asset management)
- Insurance

Yin Earth

Wealth Traits: Nurturing, service-oriented, and relational

Industries

- Hospitality (hotels, restaurants, tourism)
- Wellness (spa, mental health, alternative medicine)
- Human resources and recruitment
- Agriculture and food production
- Social work and nonprofit groups

Metal: The Value Arbitrator

Metal energy's command of the financial world is defined by ruthless precision and a discerning eye for value.

This strategic profile is for the master strategist who excels at dissecting complex systems, eliminating friction, and extracting the most profitable returns.

Its power is in the ability to refine and optimize, turning every opportunity into a polished asset.

Core Energy

Metal energy is the force of discipline, precision, and command. It represents finance, technology infrastructure, and heavy industry.

Strategic Industries and Investment Vehicles

Industries that require structure and precision align with Metal energy. This includes financial services (banking, private equity), manufacturing, cybersecurity, automotive, and military technology.

This energy thrives in environments of order and high-level control. Capital is deployed into corporate bonds, derivatives, commodities (gold, silver), and strategic acquisitions.

A methodical and discerning approach allows for commanding value in assets that require detailed analysis and impeccable timing.

Yang Metal

Wealth Traits: Hard work, structure, and determination

Industries

- Engineering and manufacturing
- Legal and compliance roles
- Technology (hardware, cybersecurity)
- Automotive and machinery
- Security and defense

Yin Metal

Wealth Traits: Refinement, luxury, and attention to detail

Industries

- Jewelry and luxury goods
- Fashion and beauty industries
- Real estate (luxury properties)
- Art dealing and fine crafts
- Financial consulting for high-net-worth individuals

Water: The Market Oracle

Water energy's strategic profile is based on foresight and a deep understanding of market flows.

It is a master of intelligence and fluid navigation, possessing a unique ability to anticipate shifts and identify hidden opportunities that others cannot.

Its power is in the ability to see the currents others cannot.

Core Energy

Water energy is the force of fluidity, communication, and strategy. It represents global trade, logistics, and intellectual insight.

Strategic Industries and Investment Vehicles

Industries that are interconnected and dynamic leverage Water energy's fluidity. This includes logistics, shipping, global trade, consulting, public relations, and legal services.

This energy is uniquely suited for navigating complex systems and influencing others from behind the scenes. Returns are optimized by investing in foreign exchange (forex), international stocks, hedge funds, and strategic partnerships that involve global commerce.

An intuitive and adaptable nature allows for finding opportunities in the flow of capital and information.

Yang Water

Wealth Traits: Visionary, adaptable, and expansive

Industries

- Logistics and transportation
- Import-export and international trade
- Shipping and maritime industries
- Travel and tourism
- Technology startups (AI, cloud solutions)

Yin Water

Wealth Traits: Strategic, resourceful, and intelligence driven

Industries

- Research and development
- Financial planning and investment analysis
- Education (academic or specialized training)
- Strategic consulting (business or management)
- Data science and analytics

II. Financial Strategy by Energetic Profile

Your financial life isn't about managing money; it's a strategic extension of your personal BaZi chart. By understanding your core energetic profile, you gain a powerful, nuanced insight into your ideal approach to wealth and investment. This is the roadmap to transforming your unique talents into your most profitable assets, allowing you to operate with uncommon ease in the complex world of finance.

From Talent to Capital: Your Energetic Financial Edge

Your personal chart reveals a powerful truth: Your most profitable ventures are perfectly in sync with your innate energetic profile. By leveraging this knowledge, you can move beyond conventional wisdom and build a financial strategy that is not only robust but also perfectly aligned with your inner strength. This is your personal roadmap to converting your unique talents into quantifiable capital.

Command Your Capital: Your Energetic Wealth Strategy

True financial mastery begins with the mastery of self. Your energetic profile provides the data-driven framework for commanding your capital. This is not a guide to quick riches, but a strategic playbook that reveals how your natural talents—whether as a creator, a leader, or an innovator—are the foundation of your most profitable ventures and your most resilient investments.

It's time to stop working for money and start architecting a life of true abundance.

Direct Resource (DR): The Investment Strategist

Wealth Paradigm

Your wealth flows from your intellectual capital. You are not a hands-on operator but a master of strategy and knowledge. Your path to abundance is by monetizing your expertise via consulting, authorship, or building a knowledge-based enterprise that commands high value.

Strategic Advantage

Your ability to meticulously research and build reliable systems allows you to create predictable, compounding wealth that is resilient to market volatility. You excel at providing intellectual capital and analysis that others can act on.

Core Risk Profile

You are naturally risk-averse. Your optimal strategy involves low-to-medium risk assets, as you gain security from stability. Your biggest pitfall is analysis paralysis, causing you to miss opportunities while waiting for perfect conditions.

Indirect Resource (IR): The Market Futurist

Wealth Paradigm

You possess a powerful, intuitive connection to emerging ideas. Your wealth is generated not through logic but through groundbreaking foresight. Your path is to architect a unique system, a disruptive methodology, or to capitalize on esoteric industries that others have yet to comprehend.

Strategic Advantage

Your powerful intuition allows you to see value where others see chaos. You have a unique ability to find and nurture unconventional ventures, making you a master of first-mover advantage and long-term trends.

Core Risk Profile

You are comfortable with ambiguity and have a high risk tolerance. Your ideal strategy involves high-risk, high-reward ventures. Your biggest pitfall is neglecting to build a stable foundation, leaving your financial security vulnerable to the inevitable downturns of a speculative market.

Friend (F): The Alliance Builder

Wealth Paradigm

Your financial legacy is inextricably linked to your ability to inspire and lead. Your abundance is unlocked through collective power, building a profitable enterprise from the ground up by unifying a team.

Strategic Advantage

Your core power lies in building and monetizing networks. You excel at forming strategic alliances, inspiring loyalty, and leveraging the combined strength of a collective to generate capital.

Core Risk Profile

You thrive on medium-to-high risk when it involves a team effort. Your greatest pitfall is over reliance on the loyalty of others, which can lead to betrayal or misaligned ventures.

Part 3 | *Chapter 8 : The Abundance Matrix: Forging Your Empire of Wealth*

Rob Wealth (RW): The Dealmaker

Wealth Paradigm

Your wealth is a direct function of your influence and competitive drive. You are a natural at leveraging social capital and forging strategic partnerships. Your path to abundance is through leading ventures, syndicating deals, and capitalizing on a vast, loyal network to gain a commanding edge.

Strategic Advantage

Your sharp competitive instinct and ability to seize opportunities make you a master dealmaker. You excel in high-stakes negotiations and have a natural genius for leveraging other people's resources to create wealth for yourself.

Core Risk Profile

You thrive on high risk and competition. Your greatest pitfall is a tendency toward overconfidence, which can lead to a miscalculation of a deal's true risk or a failure to anticipate the moves of a competitor.

Eating God (EG): The Venture Innovator

Wealth Paradigm

Your abundance is directly tied to the monetization of your intellectual and creative capital. You generate wealth by architecting platforms, products, or services that stem from your unique vision, building a business around your passions.

Strategic Advantage

Your visionary mind gives you a powerful ability to create new markets and products. You are a master of intellectual property, and your wealth is found in the scalable systems and ideas you bring to life.

Core Risk Profile

You are naturally averse to financial risk. Your greatest pitfall is overthinking or perfecting a product without bringing it to market. You must learn to overcome the fear of judgment to capitalize on your creativity.

Hurting Officer (HO): The Paradigm Shifter

Wealth Paradigm

You are built to disrupt. Your greatest financial advantage is your ability to identify inefficiencies and create new market solutions. Your wealth is not found in following trends but in pioneering them—by launching a niche business, consulting with unconventional insight, or creating new technologies that redefine an industry.

Strategic Advantage

Your uncompromising, forward-thinking mindset allows you to see flaws in existing systems. Your financial power comes from your ability to disrupt a market and provide a superior, innovative alternative.

Core Risk Profile

You are comfortable with high-risk ventures that challenge the norm. Your greatest pitfall is a tendency to alienate potential partners with your unfiltered insights, which can limit your access to capital or key alliances.

Direct Wealth (DW): The Capital Manager

Wealth Paradigm

Your core competency is in disciplined, long-term wealth management. Your financial blueprint is not built on risk but on reliability and compounding growth. You excel at accumulating capital through a stable, high-value career and the meticulous management of conservative investments.

Strategic Advantage

Your integrity and disciplined approach allow you to build a resilient financial foundation. You are a master of compounding returns, and your wealth is secured by your ability to make predictable, low-risk investments and grow them over the long term.

Core Risk Profile

You are naturally risk-averse. Your greatest pitfall is being overly cautious, which can cause you to miss out on high-growth opportunities that require a higher risk tolerance.

Indirect Wealth (IW): The High-Leverage Investor

Wealth Paradigm

You are designed for unconventional wealth accumulation. Your path to financial abundance is through astute speculation, high-leverage deals, and a knack for being in the right place at the right time. You thrive on risk, and your most profitable ventures often come from leveraging your expansive network to identify and capitalize on fleeting opportunities.

Strategic Advantage

Your intuition and comfort with ambiguity allow you to profit from market inefficiency. You have a powerful ability to identify high-leverage, high-reward ventures that others are too afraid to touch, making you a true contrarian investor.

Core Risk Profile

You thrive on high-risk, high-leverage scenarios. Your greatest pitfall is over speculation, which can lead to a quick loss of capital if your intuition is not grounded in solid due diligence.

Part 3 | *Chapter 8 : The Abundance Matrix: Forging Your Empire of Wealth*

Direct Officer: The Corporate Governor

Wealth Paradigm

Your wealth is a direct reflection of your reputation and command. You generate wealth by rising through the ranks of established institutions, holding positions of authority, and building a legacy of consistent, reliable leadership. Your financial stability is intrinsically linked to your ability to lead with integrity and discipline.

Strategic Advantage

Your professional reputation and integrity are your greatest assets. You have an unparalleled ability to bring order to chaos and build wealth through the disciplined management of large-scale systems and organizations.

Core Risk Profile

You are naturally risk-averse in a professional context. Your greatest pitfall is becoming too rigid or by the book, which can make you resistant to innovative strategies that fall outside of your established comfort zone.

Seven Killings (7K): The Crisis Master

Wealth Paradigm

Your financial path is forged in high-pressure, high-stakes environments. You are a natural leader for difficult situations, and you generate wealth by tackling challenges others would avoid. Your strategic advantage is in your courage and resilience, making you uniquely suited for leading mergers, acquisitions, or corporate transformations.

Strategic Advantage

Your ability to make decisive decisions under extreme pressure is your greatest asset. You thrive on turning around distressed assets and companies, generating outsized returns where others see only failure.

Core Risk Profile

You thrive on extreme risk. Your greatest pitfall is becoming addicted to the high-stakes environment, which can lead to burnout or impulsive decisions when not grounded in a long-term strategic plan.

Part 3 | *Chapter 8 : The Abundance Matrix: Forging Your Empire of Wealth*

The trajectory of your financial journey is no longer defined by conventional wisdom or market trends.

You now possess the ultimate financial framework—a strategic advantage that allows you to position your career and investments in perfect alignment with your core energetic structure. This creates a powerful synergy that mitigates risk and unlocks exponential value.

It's time to stop working for money and start commanding your capital. Your legacy isn't something you hope for; it's something you strategically build with profound clarity.

Chapter 9
Financial Strategy in Action

We are done with the principles. Now we look at the direct results.

We move now from theory to examining ten personal narratives where an individual's inherent energy—their passionate drive, when not managed efficiently and strategically,—becomes their single greatest financial vulnerability.

Every case study in this chapter is a story designed for instant recognition, using the potent, uniform framework: "The [Emotion] That Funds the [Pitfall]."

You are about to witness the moment your emotional habits develop an emotional relationship with money that now dictates your financial destiny.

Your greatest takeaway will be the immediacy with which this self-recognition brings profound and necessary change, transforming a known weakness into your ultimate strategic strength.

Read on and prepare to recognize the costly emotional transactions you are making every day.

Part 3 | *Chapter 9 : Financial Strategy in Action*

The FEAR That Funds the Stagnation (Investment Avoidance)

Nicholas is a high-earning software engineer, the kind of person who meticulously plans server architecture, yet his personal financial life is in total disarray. His retirement accounts are gathering dust. "I make great money," he confesses, "but every time I open my investment dashboard, I panic. The fear of choosing the 'wrong' stock makes me choose nothing at all."

Nicholas's Energetic Profile is Direct Resource (The Conservative). His passionate drive is rooted in protection and safety. This drive has curdled into an emotional relationship with money based on paralyzing distrust, in which he sees every investment not as a tool for growth, but as a potential threat. He substitutes necessary action with endless research and avoidance.

His greatest risk is not in the market but in his inaction. The protective Resource energy has created an Analysis Paralysis Loop: He cannot act until he has 100% certainty, but certainty is impossible in the market. Therefore, the perfect investment never arrives, and his energy, which is meant to preserve, instead guarantees the slow loss of wealth to inflation. His high income only funds his decision fatigue.

Based on Nicholas's BaZi chart, it is best for him not to engage in active investment or trading that requires him to make frequent decisions or time the market, as this exacerbates his inherent fear. Instead, he needs to invest solely in simple, automated funds and safe assets. This aligns with his need for security while enforcing disciplined action.

Nicholas recognized that the irony of his inaction was, in fact, his most costly financial decision. His strategic shift is automated action. He committed 80% of his savings to a broad index fund, automating the investment process monthly and removing the emotional burden entirely.

Part 3 | *Chapter 9 : Financial Strategy in Action*

The RISK That Funds the Collapse (Foundational Neglect)

Noah is a manager at a busy downtown restaurant. He views his stable income as boring, so he pumps every spare money into tiny, risky companies that might suddenly explode in value. He hates the idea of money just sitting still in a bank.

The result? Zero cash in the bank. He confesses, "If my car breaks down, I have to quickly sell a high-risk investment just to cover the repair. I'm brilliant at aiming for the biggest possible payoff, but I refuse to build a safety net."

Noah's Energetic Profile is Indirect Resource (The Exponentialist). His drive for aggressive, non-linear growth leads him directly to the pitfall of Exponential Expectation, trapping him in foundational neglect. He maximizes big, risky potential while ignoring his safety cushion. His strategy is unstable because one simple expense forces him into a panicked, bad decision.

Based on Noah's BaZi chart, the essential prerequisite for safe risk-taking is stability. He realized that his strategic advantage was his ability to spot exponential growth opportunities, but that talent was a liability until his financial foundation was secured. His strategic shift is Mandatory Foundation. He automated 25 percent of his income into ultra-safe accounts—first to fund his emergency savings, and second into simple, stable growth—and only then allowed himself to play the high-risk game with the remaining funds. To solidify his strategic shift, he separated his capital into Safety, Stable Growth, and Speculation buckets, with zero transferability from Safety to Speculation, removing the emotional impulse to liquidate the foundation. He invested his Stable Growth funds into tangible assets that require a long-term mindset and cannot be impulsively sold during a market panic.

Noah's profound realization from this shift was that true financial freedom lay not in maximizing the peak of his returns, but in securing the floor of his foundation, which made his high-risk game truly strategic for the very first time.

Part 3 | *Chapter 9 : Financial Strategy in Action*

The BETRAYAL That Funds the Loss (Affinity Reliance)

Dakota is a renowned corporate disaster recovery consultant. Her professional strength lies in her ability to organize, motivate, and direct large, stressed teams during make-or-break crises. She trusts her colleagues implicitly. In her personal finances, she mirrors this team-first approach by constantly starting high-risk, joint-investment ventures with friends, family, and new business contacts. "If my team is involved, I know it's solid," she insists.

Dakota often incurs losses from misaligned ventures due to skipping due diligence and overly relying on partners' assurances. This leads to financial setbacks when team members back out, change project scopes, or mismanage operations. "I feel like I'm cursed to be betrayed," she confesses, "but I can't imagine investing alone."

Dakota's Energetic Profile is Friend (The Reactive). Her medium-to-high risk appetite only functions when she feels she is operating within a loyal team structure. Her deep need for trusted collaboration leads her directly to the pitfall of Affinity Over-reliance. She substitutes rigorous financial diligence for faith in the people she collaborates with. Her focus on team loyalty and external passion blinds her to the technical and legal risks of the venture itself.

Based on Dakota's BaZi chart, it is best for her to focus on stable, individual investments that do not require complex, shared management. She must learn to apply her rigorous, professional crisis-management focus to her personal contracts and ventures before the team is involved.

Dakota realized her strategic advantage was in managing the technical aspects of a crisis, not in creating them internally through poor partnerships. Her strategic shift focused on two simultaneous tracks: she amplified her professional success in corporate disaster recovery and, crucially, she committed to independent due diligence and automated, low-maintenance personal investments, only engaging in team ventures after a solo, exhaustive review of all contracts.

The MISCALCULATION That Funds the Failure (Competitive Blindness)

Julia is an innovative deal maker who constantly launches ambitious, high-growth projects that thrive on major market changes. She lives to compete and win. She thrives on the idea of huge profits, believing her foresight is always superior to the market's current trajectory. "My ideas are valuable," she claims, "and I only fail because the market doesn't move fast enough to realize my genius."

The outcome? Catastrophic losses due to competitive blind spots. Julia's biggest deals crash when she fails to anticipate the counter-moves of a well-resourced competitor or when she massively over-estimates the market's appetite for her vision. Her overconfidence leads her to ignore cautionary market data and dismiss rival projects as irrelevant, resulting in deals being instantly nullified by a smarter, faster competitor.

Julia's Energetic Profile is Rob Wealth (The Over-Leverager). She is addicted to the intense, competitive setting. This leads her directly to the pitfall of Competitive Blindness and Objective Miscalculation. She bets entirely on her own competitive strength, often ignoring basic due diligence on rival innovations or the objective reality of the deal's risk profile.

Based on Julia's BaZi chart, it is best for her to focus her attention on objective, verifiable competitive analysis and on deal valuation. She needs to master the skill of raising capital from others (outside investors) without risking her own personal capital in the initial high-risk bets.

Julia realized her genius was in creating innovative, large ventures, but her overconfidence prevented her from seeing rival dangers. She made a strategic shift that was twofold: she became a master of competitive intelligence, building a team dedicated to objectively rating rival moves, and she restructured her business to earn fees and success commissions from deals, insulating her personal wealth from the market volatility she manages.

The PERFECTION That Funds the Exhaustion (Perfectionism Paralysis)

Reese is a brilliant creative director who is constantly exhausted. She pours time and savings into projects that never see the light of day. "I keep refining my art," she sighs, "because the thought of releasing something imperfect is paralyzing. I'm exhausted and my family feels neglected."

Reese's Energetic Profile is Eating God (The Refiner). She is trapped by the fear of an imperfect launch. Her need for perfection has developed an emotional relationship with money based on unpaid worth. She overthinks constantly, trading her expertise for zero financial return on unmonetized projects.

Her deepest pain is the guilt of sacrificing family time for what amounts to "artistic failure." This perfectionist drive leads her directly into the pitfall of Perfectionism Paralysis, which ensures she always trades her most valuable resource—her time—for zero financial return.

Based on Reese's BaZi chart, it is best for her not to spend time or capital on projects that cannot be sold at 80% completion. She must avoid any unpaid personal "passion" work that compromises paid deadlines. Instead, she needs to focus entirely on high-value, scope-specific professional engagements that reward efficiency and require firm deadlines. She must invest in delegation (virtual assistants or project managers) to finish tasks.

Reese realized her financial mandate must be efficient, paid expression, not exhausted vanity projects. She made a strategic shift in high-value assignments with time boxing. Channeling her output into lucrative client commissions, she began to adhere to strict deadlines that forced her creative mastery to generate targeted revenue by launching at the 80% mark.

Part 3 | *Chapter 9 : Financial Strategy in Action*

The IMAGE That Funds the Lie (Ego Debt)

Demi is a top-tier sales executive whose commission checks are completely swallowed by her lifestyle. She runs on the passionate drive to look like a winner, leading her to secure an extravagant luxury car lease and pay for constant high-end entertaining."I feel like I have to have the newest luxury SUV and host expensive client dinners," she explains. "Image is my currency, but it cancels out my commissions."

Demi's Energetic Profile is Hurting Officer (The Status Seeker). Her aggressive ego fuels her internal pressure to appear wealthy. Her emotional relationship with money is based on ego validation, causing her to ignore due diligence because her confidence feels like immunity. Her high income only funds her visible, depreciating status symbols.

Based on Demi's BaZi chart, it is best for her not to spend on highly visible, depreciating status symbols (luxury cars, high-end fashion, overly expensive office space). These only feed the liability. Instead, she needs to invest in private, income-producing assets (rental properties or equity) and pay for external analysts or due diligence experts. She must use money to conquer markets, not to impress people.

Demi realized her energy wasn't meant for being a flashy spender; it was meant for being a ruthless, calculated behind-the-scenes competitor. Her action plan is simple: stop competing to look rich and start competing to be rich. Her strategic shift is to redirected her passionate drive from buying luxury items to aggressively acquiring cash-flow assets. She implemented a financial guardrail: every single deal now requires a non-negotiable, 30-day review by an external expert. This forced waiting period acts as a cooling-off process, guaranteeing that her ego never impulsively drives a transaction that alienates key allies.

Part 3 | *Chapter 9 : Financial Strategy in Action*

The CONTROL That Funds the Opportunity Cost (Process Rigidity)

Oliver is a dedicated hospital maintenance technician whose primary financial goal is to replace his old, failing vehicle, which is essential for his work commute. He has successfully saved money for a down payment, but he refuses to visit a used car lot. Instead, he spends six months building a complex, custom-coded spreadsheet, analyzing repair frequency data from three separate auto forums. "I need to be 100% certain I've chosen the statistically best vehicle," he says.

Oliver's Energetic Profile is Direct Wealth (The Process Architect). He is trapped by the illusion that effort equals return. He has developed an emotional relationship with money based on effort-as-value. His rigidity and commitment to his self-made process results in his car finally breaking down entirely, forcing him to take expensive alternative transportation and lose hours of overtime because he missed the window to purchase a simple, reliable replacement.

He pays a heavy opportunity cost—lost income and job risk—guaranteeing his inability to leverage simple systems. The pitfall of Process Rigidity ensures he funds catastrophic failure because absolute control is more important than achieving the goal.

Based on Oliver's BaZi chart, it is best for him not to spend time on analysis that delays action or create complex systems that require constant personal oversight. Instead, he needs to invest heavily in simplicity and automation, committing capital to necessary purchases immediately when the funds are available.

Oliver realized his true financial mandate was timeliness and leverage, not perfect control. His strategic shift is systematize and simplify. He finally commited to using a third-party, single-click platform to locate and purchase a reliable vehicle within 72 hours of its initial recommendation, he proved that immediate, imperfect action was infinitely more valuable than wasted efforts on complex, non-committing research.

Part 3 | *Chapter 9 : Financial Strategy in Action*

The THRILL That Funds the Crash (The Fast Lane Fallacy)

Blake is a midlevel marketing manager with a steady income, but he finds the consistent, slow pace of saving and investing monotonous. He lives for the passionate drive of a massive, instant gain, which prevents him from establishing a reliable liquid reserve. "I saw the chance to double my net worth overnight with a meme-stock spike," he admits. "I liquidated my entire emergency fund and leveraged high-interest debt instruments to go all in. Now the bubble has burst, the savings are gone, and I'm stuck paying high-interest debt."

Blake's Energetic Profile is Indirect Wealth (The Speculator). He chases rapid spikes because steady stability feels like failure. His emotional relationship with money is based on maximal-exposure recklessness. He uses private resources, often from debt or critical funds, to chase volatile ventures, driven by a need for the adrenaline rush of a massive win.

He avoids the stable base that would protect him from his own unrestrained brilliance, guaranteeing repeated fiscal ruin. This emotional pattern traps him in the pitfall of No Safety Net—what we call The Fast Lane Fallacy.

Based on Blake's BaZi chart, it is best for him not to use core savings or debt (borrowed capital or home equity) to fund risk-laden ventures where he is the sole risk-bearer. Instead, he needs to build secure, cash-flowing assets (real estate, stable dividends) first, then monetize his foresight through consulting, separating his exciting ideas from his stable capital.

Blake realized his inherent talent was in foresight and strategy, not in personally bearing the risk of capital loss. His strategic shift is fee-for-foresight. He implemented a hands-off, low-risk savings plan, he shifted his career to building complex risk models for large institutions for fixed retainers, monetizing the chaos he saw without direct loss.

Part 3 | *Chapter 9 : Financial Strategy in Action*

The FEAR That Funds the Freeze (Financial Compliance Trap)

Parker is the Chief Compliance Officer at a large investment firm whose professional success is built on his department's absolute adherence to every letter of the law and regulatory statute. While his strict dedication has been effective in preventing regulatory fines in the past, it has made the firm dangerously slow to adapt to the new, complex regulatory environment. The firm is hemorrhaging money on outdated, manual audit processes that take weeks to complete. "I cannot be responsible for certifying a system that hasn't been validated by a multi-year audit, even if our current costs are financially unsustainable."

Parker's Energetic Profile is Direct Officer (The Rule-Bound). He is trapped by the intense fear of being out of compliance with the pre-existing rule, which has led to paralysis. His passionate drive for structure has resulted in an emotional attachment to the existing written protocol, where the method is valued more than the desired outcome. Parker's financial ruin is the massive operational waste and the loss of market share resulting from this paralysis. He is convinced his value lies in flawless procedural preservation, leading him to resist technology that would improve compliance while dramatically cutting costs.

Based on Parker's BaZi chart, it is best for him to shift his focus from merely enforcing old rules to creating and sanctioning necessary new frameworks. He needs to dedicate resources to controlled digital transformation, such as building automated systems for the future of regulatory efficiency, not just manually enforcing the rules of the past.

Parker realized that his inherent talent was not in following rules, but in governing the change of rules. His strategic shift is The Compliance Bridge. He transformed his role into the Head of Regulatory Modernization, using his deep knowledge of current law to draft and pilot the new internal policies that safely incorporate AI tools, merging his love of rigid compliance with the necessity of financial security and efficiency.

The INTENSITY That Funds the Chaos (Sudden Financial Eruption)

Lane is a driven project leader whose financial life is marked by sudden, dramatic, and costly non-negotiable decisions. "I get an internal signal—a kind of intense urgency—and I have to act now," she explains. "Last month, I impulsively bought a second property simply because I was tired of my current neighborhood, without selling the first one. Now I'm burdened by two mortgages and massive closing fees. I act, then I pay for the poor planning."

Lane's Energetic Profile is 7 Killing (The Decisive Force). She is driven by a profound need for immediate, decisive action. She developed an emotional relationship with money based on immediate gratification. Her inability to tolerate internal friction causes her to act aggressively on large financial matters, leading to huge penalties and loss of capital due to haste. This dynamic traps her in the pitfall of Sudden Financial Eruption, draining her wealth by eliminating all due diligence. Lane's financial ruin comes from the impulsive commitment of large capital without proper planning, leading to massive financial drag.

Based on Lane's BaZi chart, it is best for her not to make any large financial or career decisions within 72 hours of the thought appearing. She must never use high-interest debt to fund an immediate impulse. Instead, she needs to invest her capital to low-friction, high-impact ventures. She must monetize her intensity, not act on it personally.

Lane realized her strategic advantage was high-impact force, but she needed to channel it through calculated strategy. Her strategic shift is The 72-Hour Filter. She implemented a non-negotiable, 72-hour delay on all major financial decisions, requiring the immediate filing of paperwork with a financial advisor (her filter) to enforce the cooling-off period.

Part 3 | *Chapter 9 : Financial Strategy in Action*

You have now walked through ten financial journeys, and perhaps you've seen your own reflection in several of these powerful accounts. The essential truth of this chapter is that recognition is half the transformation. By identifying the exact root cause—the specific emotional relationship with money your passionate drive created when mismanaged—you instantly gain the mental awareness required to stop the loss. The liability is no longer a mystery. It is a fixed target.

The BaZi directives provided in these case studies are not general tips. They are the non-negotiable financial boundaries designed specifically to counteract your energetic profile's most costly impulses. Take these strategic do's and don'ts to heart.

When you fully accept your story, you achieve The CLARITY Moment—the pivotal shift where the decision to change becomes faster and easier than the pain of staying the same. You are now ready to formalize your financial mandate and execute your strategic shift.

Part 4
The Blueprint for Relationships

Harmony is an active, effortless flow you can strategically cultivate.

This part of the book is where strategic clarity meets your deepest emotional life.

By mastering the energetic flow of your intimate, personal and professional bonds, you gain the ability to heal old wounds, eliminate repeating conflicts, and fundamentally change your destiny.

This is the ultimate application of BaZi: creating a powerful environment where every connection is not just stable, but also becomes a source of dynamic energy, profound emotional security, and true abundance that fuels every other area of your life—from your health to your wealth.

By mastering the insights in this section, you will learn to move with clarity in your relationships, achieving a state of equilibrium that transforms your partnerships into your greatest strategic asset.

Chapter 10
The Relational Profiles – Your Energetic Code for Love

Your BaZi chart is the ultimate tool for decoding and commanding the dynamics of human connection. It extends far beyond career and finance to provide a profound framework for understanding and mastering the flow of love.

By understanding your unique relational tendencies and those of others, you can transform friction into empathy and strategically architect deeper, more resilient bonds.

By aligning the Ten Energetic Profiles with the different emotional languages of communication—verbal appreciation, thoughtful actions, meaningful presents, shared moments, and affectionate contact—you will gain strategic insight into your most valuable assets: your love life.

This chapter is your guide to unlocking your code and building powerful, aligned partnerships based on profound clarity.

Direct Resource (DR) Profile: The Resilient Anchor

Emotional Communication Style: Thoughtful Actions and Shared Moments

How DR Profile Expresses Love

Your love is built on intellectual support and a profound sense of security. You express affection by offering wise counsel and a calm, stable presence. You cherish meaningful conversations and value a partner who appreciates your thoughtful and dependable nature.

How DR Profile Wants to Receive Love

To foster a deeper bond, focus on consistent, unwavering support. Your partner feels most secure when you provide a stable, calm anchor in their life.

Love Blind Spots of DR Profile

You may be so focused on stability and consistency that you seem passive. Your partner may feel you are not actively engaged in the relationship if you don't initiate or show passion.

Indirect Resource (IR) Profile: The Intuitive Companion

Emotional Communication Style: Shared Moments and Affectionate Contact

How IR Profile Expresses Love

Your love is unconventional and deeply intuitive. You express affection through your presence and a profound understanding that often transcends words. You value intimate moments of shared understanding.

How IR Profile Wants to Receive Love

To build powerful bonds, communicate your love through nonverbal cues and intuitive understanding. Your partner feels seen when you show you understand their inner world without a need for explanation.

Love Blind Spots of IR Profile

Your intuitive nature can lead you to withdraw and assume your partner understands your needs without being told. This can create a lack of clear communication and relational friction.

Friend (F) Profile: The Independent Ally

Emotional Communication Style: Thoughtful Actions and Shared Moments

How F Profile Expresses Love

Your love is a bond of mutual respect and partnership. You express affection through a sense of camaraderie and by doing things side by side. You value shared activities and a relationship built on loyalty and teamwork.

How F Profile Wants to Receive Love

To cultivate a deeper connection, focus on creating shared experiences and goals. Your partner feels most loved when you are a trusted and equal teammate in their life.

Love Blind Spots of F Profile

Your focus on independence can sometimes make you seem distant or uninterested in deep emotional intimacy. You must make space for vulnerability and not see every interaction as a team-based exercise.

Rob Wealth (RW) Profile: The Charismatic Partner

Emotional Communication Style: Verbal Appreciation and Meaningful Presents

How RW Profile Expresses Love

Your love is a dynamic pursuit. You express affection through generous praise and a focus on shared ambition. You value recognition and appreciate a partner who celebrates your achievements and drive.

How RW Profile Wants to Receive Love

To create a powerful bond, strategically validate your partner with sincere words of admiration and by including them in your high-stakes world. You strengthen your connection by making them a part of your success.

Love Blind Spots of RW Profile

Your competitive drive can sometimes create a dynamic of winning and losing within the relationship. You must learn to separate your life from your professional pursuits to avoid friction.

Eating God (EG) Profile: The Nurturing Visionary

Emotional Communication Style: Verbal Appreciation and Shared Moments

How EG Profile Expresses Love

Your love is a creative expression. You express affection through sincere praise, encouragement, and a genuine interest in your partner's inner world. You value shared experiences where you can connect on a deep, emotional level.

How EG Profile Wants to Receive Love

To establish a deeper connection, create an environment of genuine care and creativity. Your partner feels most loved when you show unconditional support for their dreams and passions.

Love Blind Spots of EG Profile

You can become so focused on nurturing your partner that you neglect your own needs. You must learn to set boundaries and prioritize your own well-being to avoid burnout and codependency.

Hurting Officer (HO) Profile: The Discerning Catalyst

Emotional Communication Style: Verbal Appreciation and Thoughtful Actions

How HO Profile Expresses Love

Your love is a discerning intellectual exchange. You express affection by offering unique, insightful compliments and by proving your competence. You desire a partner who can acknowledge and praise your brilliant, unconventional mind.

How HO Profile Wants to Receive Love

To initiate a powerful bond, engage your partner with insightful conversation and challenge them to grow. Your partner feels most valued when you respect and admire their intellect and capacity for change.

Love Blind Spots of HO Profile

Your unfiltered honesty can be perceived as harsh or critical, creating relational friction. You must learn to soften your approach and recognize that not every insight should be delivered with brutal directness.

Direct Wealth (DW) Profile: The Steadfast Provider

Emotional Communication Style: Thoughtful Actions and Meaningful Presents

How DW Profile Expresses Love

Your love is built on reliability and commitment. You demonstrate affection by being dependable, providing stability, and taking care of practical matters. You show you care through consistent, tangible efforts.

How DW Profile Wants to Receive Love

To develop a powerful bond, focus on being a rock of stability and consistency. Your partner feels most secure when you honor your commitments and create a reliable, safe environment.

Love Blind Spots of DW Profile

Your methodical and practical approach may be interpreted as a lack of emotional spontaneity or passion. Remember to express your love in ways that are emotionally resonant, not just transactional.

Part 4 | Chapter 10 : The Relational Profiles – Your Energetic Code for Love

Indirect Wealth (IW) Profile: The Generous Trailblazer

Emotional Communication Style: Meaningful Presents and Verbal Appreciation

How IW Profile Expresses Love

Your love is a passionate adventure. You express affection through grand gestures and with your playful, generous nature. You value a partner who is spontaneous and appreciates the thrill of the unexpected.

How IW Profile Wants to Receive Love

To instill a powerful bond, use grand, romantic gestures to show your devotion. Your partner feels most loved when you bring excitement and generosity into their life.

Love Blind Spots of IW Profile

Your adventurous nature may be perceived as a lack of seriousness or commitment. Learn to balance spontaneity with consistent, reliable affection to build trust.

Direct Officer (DO) Profile: The Principled Balancer

Emotional Communication Style: Verbal Appreciation and Thoughtful Actions

How DO Profile Expresses Love

Your love is built on principles of honor and respect. You express affection through a sense of duty, protection, and sincere praise. You value a partner who respects your boundaries and the order you bring to the relationship.

How DO Profile Wants to Receive Love

To nurture a powerful bond, create a sense of structure, safety, and respect. Your partner feels most secure when they know you are an honorable and protective force in their life.

Love Blind Spots of DO Profile

Your rigid sense of duty can be perceived as controlling or cold. Learn to express your love with more emotional warmth and flexibility, and allow for more spontaneity and vulnerability.

Part 4 | *Chapter 10 : The Relational Profiles – Your Energetic Code for Love*

Seven Killings (7K) Profile: The Relentless Champion

Emotional Communication Style: Verbal Appreciation and Affectionate Contact

How 7K Profile Expresses Love

Your love is a commanding force of passion and protection. You express affection through intense loyalty, unwavering support, and a desire to be a champion for your partner. You value a partner who is strong and capable and who can match your intensity.

How 7K Profile Wants to Receive Love

To architect a powerful bond, focus on being a relentless force for your partner's success and well-being. Your partner feels most loved when you fight for their dreams and protect their interests.

Love Blind Spots of 7K Profile

Your intensity can sometimes be overwhelming or feel like control. Learn to dial back the intensity and give your partner space to lead, ensuring the relationship is a partnership and not a pursuit.

Chapter 11
Mastering Relational Friction

Your energetic framework is the ultimate tool for proactively commanding dynamics. Moving beyond mere understanding, this section provides a strategic approach to not only anticipate but transform your most common challenges into your greatest strengths.

This is not about mitigating friction; it's about architecting resilience, providing you with guidance to turning every obstacle into an opportunity for a deeper, more powerful bond.

Direct Resource (DR) Profile: The Challenge of Detachment

Your tendency to overthink and analyze can lead to a passive role in the relationship. You may appear aloof or disengaged, as you're often processing emotions internally instead of actively participating in the emotional exchange.

How to Navigate

Consciously bridge the emotional gap. Set a daily intention to ask a key person in your life about their day and actively listen. Consciously share a feeling or thought you have, even if it feels small, to demonstrate your engagement and show them that their experience is valued.

The Strategic Win

By actively participating in emotional exchange, you transform from a passive observer into a relational anchor, a source of unwavering intellectual and emotional security.

Indirect Resource (IR) Profile: The Emotional Misfire

You can struggle with verbalizing your emotions, leading to frequent misunderstandings with clients, teammates, or family. Your intuitive and unconventional nature may make it difficult for others to understand your feelings or intentions, creating a sense of emotional distance.

How to Navigate

Master creative outlets to express yourself. Write a heartfelt letter, share a song that reminds you of them, or use a visual presentation to convey your complex feelings or unconventional insights. Where words fail, these unique gestures can speak volumes and deepen your professional or personal connection.

The Strategic Win

By finding your unique voice, you turn potential emotional misfires into a unique language of connection, forging a deep, unspoken bond that others cannot replicate.

Friend (F) Profile: The Vulnerability Barrier

Your fierce independence can be perceived by partners, siblings, or direct reports as a reluctance to be vulnerable or to fully commit to the relationship's shared vision. While you value partnership, you may unintentionally push others away by prioritizing your personal freedom and space.

How to Navigate

Strategically share your vulnerabilities. Initiate conversations with a trusted ally about your fears, hopes, and deeper emotions concerning a shared goal or project. This builds intimacy and shows them that they are a trusted and essential part of your core self.

The Strategic Win

You transform your independence from a barrier into a pillar of trust, creating a powerful partnership where your autonomy and commitment are both celebrated.

Rob Wealth (RW) Profile: The Validation Trap

Your competitive drive and need for validation can manifest as a tendency to compare your team's performance, your sibling's achievements, or your partner's success to others. You may unconsciously seek external validation for your relationship or shared project, which can lead to insecurity and a lack of true internal intimacy.

How to Navigate

Redirect your competitive energy toward a shared goal with your key relational counterpart (partner, boss, or team). Work as a team to achieve a common objective, and celebrate your shared wins to build a "you and me against the world" mentality.

The Strategic Win

Move from seeking external validation to commanding internal power, creating a dynamic where your greatest achievements are the ones you build together.

Eating God (EG) Profile: The Avoidance of Conflict

Your need for harmony and intellectual connection can lead to passive-aggression when your emotional needs go unmet by family or coworkers. You may withdraw instead of directly communicating your frustrations, creating unspoken tension in your home or professional environment.

How to Navigate

Your path to resolution is through direct, yet gentle, communication. Use "I feel" statements to express your needs without blame, and proactively schedule quality time or collaborative sessions to ensure you feel emotionally and intellectually connected.

The Strategic Win

By mastering direct communication, you transform your passive energy into a force of creative clarity, ensuring your relationships are both harmonious and authentically fulfilling.

Hurting Officer (HO) Profile: The Critical Analyst

Your insightful and analytical nature can manifest as overly critical and blunt communication. You may unintentionally create conflict by disregarding emotional diplomacy, prioritizing intellectual honesty over sensitivity.

How to Navigate

Before speaking, pause and ask yourself, "Is this kind? Is this necessary?" Frame your insights as constructive observations rather than absolute criticisms, and practice empathy by considering the other person's emotional state before offering your analysis.

The Strategic Win

You transform your critical mind into a catalyst for growth, using your powerful insights to help your relational circle and your relationship evolve without sacrificing empathy.

Direct Wealth (DW) Profile: The Rigidity Trap

Your need for stability and routine can be perceived as rigidity or an unwillingness to adapt by colleagues, family or partners. This can lead to others feeling bored or emotionally disconnected, as they may desire more spontaneity and adventure in a project or personal setting.

How to Navigate

To maintain harmony, intentionally schedule moments of spontaneity. Agree to an "adventure night" with a partner once a month or surprise your team with an unplanned creative problem-solving session to show you value their need for excitement while still preserving your need for security.

The Strategic Win

You turn your rigidity into a strategic framework for spontaneity, proving that a disciplined life can also be a life of rich, intentional experience for everyone involved.

Indirect Wealth (IW) Profile: The Commitment Conundrum

Your spontaneous nature and need for excitement can lead to a lack of commitment or a restless demeanor with long-term projects, business plans, or partners. Your desire for continuous stimulation may make it difficult to settle into a stable, long-term partnership or career path.

How to Navigate

Channel your energy into building a shared vision with a partner, boss or team. By working together toward a long-term goal—like starting a business or completing a challenging project—you can satisfy your need for adventure and risk-taking within the bounds of a committed relationship.

The Strategic Win

You transform your restlessness into a force for shared ambition, proving that true excitement lies not in constantly new experiences but in a life built and conquered together.

Direct Officer (DO) Profile: The Unyielding Idealist

Your principled nature can become inflexible and overly judgmental. You may impose your high standards on your subordinates, siblings, or partner, creating an environment of criticism and dissatisfaction when they don't meet your expectations.

How to Navigate

Focus on managing your own expectations rather than trying to control the actions of others. Practice giving affirmations and praise for their efforts and recognize that perfection is not a prerequisite for a fulfilling partnership or effective team.

The Strategic Win

You transform your idealism from a source of friction into a source of inspiration, leading with principled action while allowing others the freedom to forge their own path under your strategic guidance.

Seven Killings (7K) Profile: The Unrelenting Executor

Your intensity and action-oriented nature can be overwhelming, leading you to create unnecessary conflict or drama with colleagues or family. You may overcorrect for perceived threats, causing others to feel like they're in a constant battle and are unable to relax around you.

How to Navigate

Learn to temper your passion with patience. Practice mindful reflection to determine if a perceived threat is a real challenge or a response to your own internal stress. Not every challenge in a relationship or project requires a fight.

The Strategic Win

You transform your intensity from a source of friction into a force for powerful growth, using your relentless drive to overcome real-world obstacles and create a life of secure victory for everyone you lead or love.

Chapter 12
Nurturing Your Connections

Successfully navigating relationships is more than just identifying challenges; it's about proactively implementing a strategic framework for growth and harmony.

A Strategic Framework for Deeper Bonds

1. **Understand their blueprint** – The key to true empathy is to see beyond the other person's actions and understand their core energetic profile. By recognizing their energetic structure, you can perceive their behaviors as a natural expression of their profile, not a personal attack. This shifts your perspective from judgment to understanding.

2. **Align your emotional communication style** – Your knowledge of their energetic profile is the definitive guide to their primary emotional communication style. For example, a Direct Wealth individual, who values security, will likely respond to another person who demonstrates thoughtful actions rather than one who shows verbal appreciation. By aligning your efforts with what they truly value, you ensure that your emotional investments yield maximum returns.

3. **Communicate strategically** – Tailor your communication style to their energetic profile. Be direct and concise with a Seven Killings partner, but use diplomacy and nuance with a Hurting Officer. Adjusting your approach mitigates friction and ensures your message is received and understood as intended.

4. **Manage conflict proactively** – The most powerful strategy is to anticipate friction before it occurs. Use your combined energetic profiles to predict potential friction points. For example, a partnership between a Direct Wealth (stability) and an Indirect Wealth (risk) will require proactive, honest discussions about financial boundaries and goals to avoid future conflict.

By applying this strategic framework, you move beyond simple communication and begin to develop a legacy of truly resilient and harmonious connections. This is the ultimate definitive strategy in your personal life.

Chapter 13
The Relational Profiles in Action - Case Studies

Your personal chart is the most powerful resource for building a life of profound love and connection, spanning your most intimate, familial and professional bonds.

This is where theory meets reality. The following case studies—featuring CEOs, siblings, marriage partners, managers, and employees serve as your guide, illuminating the real-world dynamics of love, conflict, and harmony.

They show you how to transform relational friction into a deeper bond and cultivate your most valuable legacy: your ability to move with clarity in every relationship that matters.

Part 4 | *Chapter 13 : The Relational Profiles in Action - Case Studies*

Case Study: Grace

Ms. Grace, a successful architect with a Direct Resource (DR) profile, came to me exhausted. Her relationship with her 16-year-old daughter, Luna, had become a war zone. Grace's life revolves around structure, academic excellence, and providing the "best"—the DR way. Luna, a Hurting Officer (HO) profile, is a brilliant artist, but is constantly pushing back against authority, skipping traditional homework for radical art projects, and sees her mother's help as smothering criticism.

"I provide everything a good mother should—tutors, stability, healthy food—but she treats me like the enemy! She is brilliant, but she's throwing away her future. I feel so unappreciated and helpless to guide her."

Grace's overwhelming need to nourish and control was inadvertently stifling Luna's need for creative expression and freedom. Her love felt like a heavy, immovable mountain. Luna is the star of genius and non-conformity. She needs to articulate her unique vision.

I instructed Grace to pivot her Resource from control to support. Instead of questioning the what (the art), she should focus her energy on the how (providing structured resources for her art).

Grace established a "Creative Sanctuary" in the house where her rules did not apply. She used her Direct Resource to fund a specialized art mentorship and provided professional-grade materials, acknowledging that her role was to supply the high-quality environment, not dictate the artistic outcome.

The shift allowed Luna to feel respected, instantly lowering her defensiveness. Grace transformed their relational friction into a supportive, deeper bond that honored her daughter's genius.

Part 4 | *Chapter 13 : The Relational Profiles in Action - Case Studies*

Case Study: Harry

Mr. Harry, the creative visionary with an Indirect Resource (IR) profile, was losing sleep. His business partner, Ms. Ava, the finance lead, a Direct Wealth (DW) profile, was threatening to pull funding. Harry thrives on intuition, research, and non-traditional ideas but is weak on execution and schedules. Ava demands measurable results, predictable income, and sees Harry's intellectual curiosity as a costly, time-wasting distraction.

"She constantly rejects my most innovative ideas because they don't have a spreadsheet attached! I feel my genius is being suffocated by her obsession with 'the bottom line.' We're making money, but she's preventing the true leap."

Harry lacks discipline and can procrastinate on the practical steps needed to monetize ideas, giving the partner no proof of concept. Ava is masterful at structure, consistency, and protecting stable, predictable income streams.

I showed Harry that Ava wasn't resisting innovation; it was resisting risk without clarity. Her need for measurable stability was the essential container for his ungrounded ideas.

Harry agreed to dedicate the first two days of every week to methodically document his insights into friendly formats: timelines, budgets, and clear KPIs. Ava, in turn, committed to allocating a small "Sandbox Fund" for Harry to test his non-traditional ideas without immediate scrutiny.

The partnership transformed from constant conflict to a synergistic flow, generated the complex, unique insights, and provided the rigorous, predictable structure needed to monetize them ethically and sustainably.

Case Study: Luis

Luis, the son with a Friend (F) profile, consulted me about the financial strain caused by his father. Luis is generous, loyal, and values his social network above all else. His father, an Indirect Wealth (IW) profile—sharp, opportunistic, and a risk-taker who frequently needs emergency loans from Luis for new, volatile ventures. Luis feels guilty for saying no, but his own finances are suffering.

"I feel terrible because my dad is my best friend. He always says, 'just one more big push,' but his ventures are always high-risk. I just want to support him, but he keeps jeopardizing my stability, he is constantly moving assets."

Luis struggles to create firm personal boundaries, particularly with close connections, allowing his resources to be eroded by unpredictable needs. The Father is a master of leverage and seeing profit where others see risk. However, it can see money as merely a tool for opportunity, not security.

I helped Luis see that being a Friend did not mean being a perpetual bank. Luis needed to use his Friend energy to find non-monetary support solutions.

Luis was advised to use his network to find the father better resources (e.g., connecting him with venture capitalists or financial advisors) rather than providing capital himself. He established a clear, non-negotiable financial boundary, and substituted emotional support and network connections for cash.

Luis maintained his close relationship by affirming his loyalty but protected his resources by changing the nature of his support. He gained financial clarity and taught his father, by example, how to use networks strategically instead of relying on emotional leverage.

Part 4 | *Chapter 13 : The Relational Profiles in Action - Case Studies*

Case Study: Anya

Anya, the daughter with an Eating God (EG) profile, was struggling to communicate with her father, who is a Seven Killings (7K) profile. Anya is artistic, loves comfort, values freedom, and produces excellent work over time. Her father is a high-ranking military official—fierce, demanding, obsessed with deadlines, and views Anya's relaxed pace as a weakness.

"He sees my pace as laziness and my need for comfort as a failure. I just want to enjoy my work and my life, but his intense pressure makes me freeze up. I feel sick every time I have to report my progress to him."

Anya can become too passive, indulging in comfort and procrastination, especially when faced with extreme pressure.

The Father with the warrior energy—forces things to completion, handles crises, and demands extreme accountability.

I advised Anya to stop resisting pressure and instead, strategically redirect its force. Anya was instructed to use her creative energy—to provide her father with a weekly "Strategic Digest." This was a short, aesthetically pleasing report detailing her long-term plan and proving her productivity, satisfying the father's need for strict, documented control and accountability.

By creating a polished output that fed his father's need for control, Anya neutralized the friction. She transformed the relationship from a pressure cooker into a reciprocal dynamic where her gentle, artistic production was respected, and his discipline was channeled into supporting her strategic growth.

Part 4 | *Chapter 13 : The Relational Profiles in Action - Case Studies*

Case Study: Charlotte

Charlotte, the sister with a Hurting Officer (HO) profile, approached me because her relationship with her brother, a successful corporate security executive with a Seven Killings (7K) profile, was toxic. Charlotte needs creative freedom, hates structure, and sees the world as needing improvement. Her brother is obsessed with order, discipline, and sees Charlotte's creative chaos as an unnecessary risk and expense. Every conversation turns into a power struggle.

"He treats me like a subordinate he needs to control, constantly criticizing my career choices and finances. His pressure completely shuts down my creativity. I just want him to respect my space and genius."

Charlotte can be overly sensitive to criticism and can destroy its own rules unnecessarily, leading to self-sabotage and financial instability. The brother has a strong sense of discipline and crisis management. It sees potential threats clearly, which is a valuable protective force.

I instructed Charlotte to strategically redirect her energy. Instead of using it to critique her brother's control, she was to use her genius to create a perfectly ordered defense of her own life. She was advised to present him with an unsolicited, impeccable, professional-grade business plan for her next creative venture, satisfying his need for structure and accountability.

Charlotte used her brilliance to create a detailed, visual, strategic document. By proactively feeding his need for control, she disarmed his criticism.

Charlotte transformed her brother's energy from a critic into an accountability partner. She gained the freedom and respect she craved by supplying the clarity output that her brother's profile required, thus achieving relational harmony.

Case Study: Ethan

Mr. Ethan, the elder brother with a Direct Wealth (DW) profile, consulted me about severe tension with his younger brother, who is a Direct Officer (DO) profile. Ethan values stable, dependable income, budgeting, and tangible resources. His younger brother is obsessed with reputation, status, and following rigid, established family and social protocols, which Ethan finds financially illogical and stifling.

"Every major decision—from cars to schools—has to be about 'what people think,' not 'what we can actually afford'. He wants prestige, and I'm the one who has to structure the budget and deal with the predictable expenses. He's destroying my hard-earned stability."

Ethan can be overly focused on tangibles and resistance to spending on anything without clear, immediate monetary return, missing the value of reputation and influence. The younger Brother excels at maintaining status, authority, and public respect, which are essential for long-term influence and safety.

I showed Ethan that his brother was simply protecting their family's reputational wealth—a vital asset for Ethan. The conflict arose because Ethan wasn't effectively financing the brother's goals.

Ethan was instructed to change his language from expense to investment. He agreed to strategically allocate a fixed, separate "Budget" for status-enhancing items, giving his brother control over a resource for the family's reputation. This satisfied the brother's need for authority without jeopardizing Ethan's overall budget.

By understanding the brother's energy as a protective force, Ethan transformed the argument over spending into a mutual strategy for long-term asset protection.

Part 4 | *Chapter 13 : The Relational Profiles in Action - Case Studies*

Case Study: Lily

Ms. Lily, a manager with an Indirect Resource (IR) profile, sought guidance regarding her charismatic but demanding boss, who is a strong Rob Wealth (RW) profile. Lily is intuitive, excels at deep research, and needs time alone to process data. Her boss thrives on team collaboration, urgent group activity, and public praise, constantly interrupting Lily's focus for mandatory, often chaotic, group meetings.

"I feel mentally depleted because she won't leave me alone to do the deep work. She sees my need for quiet focus as laziness, and her constant group meetings destroy my concentration. I can't think clearly in that environment."

Lily can become too isolated in her intellectual bubble, making its vital knowledge inaccessible or unapplied, which the boss interprets as a lack of effort. The Boss is highly effective at mobilizing large teams, creating communal energy, and achieving success through collective effort.

I showed Lily that the boss needs to see visible, shared contributions. Lily was advised to strategically package her solitary research for team consumption.

Lily established a ritual of providing a short, impactful "Insight Brief" before the team meetings, demonstrating her solitary work in a visible way that the boss could celebrate and distribute. She then proactively scheduled short, non-negotiable "deep work blocks" in her calendar, which the boss, seeing her commitment, learned to respect.

Lily successfully protected her focus time while achieving greater recognition. She transformed the friction into a flow where her independent thought fueled the team's collective success, leading to greater respect.

Part 4 | *Chapter 13 : The Relational Profiles in Action - Case Studies*

Case Study: Emily

Ms. Emily, the younger sister with an Indirect Wealth (IW) profile, came in due to frustration with her older sister, who is a Direct Resource (DR) profile. Emily is opportunistic, flexible, and thrives on leveraging risk. Her older sister is highly stable, cautious, and criticizes Emily's "risky gambles," constantly offering unsolicited advice rooted in tradition and safety.

"She treats me like a child! I built my fortune through smart risk, but all she sees is danger. Her constant lectures make me question my own judgment and derail my focus. I just want her to stop trying to 'save' me."

Sofia can be overly exposed to risk and is sometimes dismissive of the foundational importance of safety and rules, which worries the Older sibling. The older Sister provides unwavering emotional and physical support and security. It is the essential safety net.

I helped Emily understand that her sister's criticism was not judgment; it was simply her primary expression of love—the overwhelming need to nourish and protect.

Emily was advised to strategically feed her sister's energy. She started proactively asking her sister for non-financial advice (like health, nutrition, or home stability) and genuinely implemented it. By consciously creating a space where the sister felt needed and effective, Emily lowered the sister's critical energy directed at her finances.

By acknowledging the sister's need to nurture, Emily satisfied her sister's protective instinct. She preserved her financial independence while transforming their friction into a more accepting, structurally sound relationship, achieving relational harmony.

Part 4 | *Chapter 13 : The Relational Profiles in Action - Case Studies*

Case Study: Diana

Ms. Diana, the older spouse with an Eating God (EG) profile, consulted me about a growing distance in her marriage. Diana is a gentle soul, focused on enjoying the refined arts, comfort, and deep philosophical exploration. Her partner, a Friend (F) profile, is highly social, needs constant group activity, and struggles to understand Diana's need for quiet introspection and alone time.

"I feel guilty for needing my space and she feels rejected when I don't want to go to every social gathering. We are spending less quality time together, and she can't grasp that my slow, quiet hobbies are actually productive and essential for my happiness."

Diana can become too passive and self-indulgent, often failing to communicate its deep emotional needs in a way that others can act on. The Partner is characterized by loyalty, excellent social cohesion, and the ability to mobilize resources and support through networks.

I showed Diana that her partner's energy wasn't rejecting her; it was simply seeking a shared experience. The solution was to blend their energies proactively.

Diana was advised to strategically apply her energy's refined taste to her partner's social agenda. Instead of resisting the social events, she agreed to attend one social event per week, provided she could curate the activity (e.g., hosting a small, artistic dinner party instead of a large, loud bar night). She also set a non-negotiable "Me Time" daily for solitary comfort.

Diana used her elegant taste to elevate their shared social life, making it more meaningful for both of them. This transformation brought greater mutual respect, transforming the emotional distance into a marriage built on shared, quality experiences and renewed marital clarity.

Cultivating a Legacy of Connection

You now possess a powerful framework for navigating the most complex and rewarding part of your life: your relationship. These case studies prove that your energetic blueprint is not a limitation but a strategic advantage. You have the power to move beyond reactive behaviors and create proactive, intentional connections.

The goal is no longer to hope for a perfect relationship, but to forge one with purpose. By understanding your own energy and decoding the blueprints of those you love, you can transform relational friction into empathy, and simple moments into a profound, shared legacy.

It's time to leverage your knowledge and build a life rich with harmony, connection, and love. Your most valuable assets are ready for your command.

Part 5
The Blueprint for Health

You've built your financial legacy and cultivated powerful relationships. But in the high-stakes world you operate in, your most critical asset is your own vitality.

This part of your Destiny Blueprint is where you will learn to align your body's unique energetic rhythm with your ambitious drive. This isn't about simply avoiding burnout; it's about intentionally designing a state of physical and emotional endurance that fuels your life.

By mastering your health, you will finally achieve the sustainable energy required to move with clarity through every aspect of your life.

Part 5 | *Chapter 14 : The Elemental Guide to Well-Being*

Chapter 14
The Elemental Guide to Well-Being

Your body is a high-performance enterprise, and its health is not a passive state but the ultimate competitive advantage. This chapter is your authoritative resource to understanding its core operating system.

Using the wisdom of BaZi, you will learn to read the energetic blueprint that governs your well-being, moving beyond conventional wellness into a state of proactive command.

True vitality is a strategic equation. The insights ahead will guide you in managing your internal ecosystem by identifying and addressing two critical states: the excessive element that demands release, and the deficient element that requires strategic nurturing.

This is your playbook for mastering the delicate equilibrium that fuels resilience, sharpens your focus, and sustains peak performance. By commanding your internal environment with purpose and precision, you unlock the capacity to operate at the highest level and secure a legacy of sustained vitality.

Wood: Pulse of Growth

Your Wood element is the powerful engine of your body, governing the liver, gallbladder, and muscular system.

Its associated emotion is anger, which, when channeled constructively, transforms into assertiveness, ambition, and the relentless drive to innovate.

Recognizing Imbalance: The Signals of Stagnation

When your Wood energy is imbalanced, your system sends clear signals of stagnation or overextension.

Physically, this manifests as persistent headaches, migraines, unexplained neck and shoulder tension, or muscle stiffness.

Emotionally, you may experience an undercurrent of resentment to irritability, or be prone to sudden, uncontrolled outbursts of anger.

These are not mere symptoms; they are red flags from your internal command center, indicating blockage in the flow of your body's vital energy.

Part 5 | *Chapter 14 : The Elemental Guide to Well-Being*

Wood: Strategic Solutions

To strategically nurture your Wood element and restore its powerful flow, deploy the following:

- **Diet** – Command your internal ecosystem with a diet rich in green, leafy vegetables, sour foods like lemons, and chlorophyll-dense superfoods. These nutrient-rich ingredients act as catalysts for detoxification, helping clear your body's channels and promote optimal energy flow.

- **Activity** – Your body needs dynamic movement to release pent-up energy. Engage in flowing activities like yoga, tai chi, or high-intensity interval training (HIIT). These exercises are a strategic way to release tension, promote flexibility, and ensure your system is operating at peak performance.

- **Lifestyle** – The most powerful remedy lies in managing your internal emotional landscape. Spend time in natural environments—particularly forests—to reconnect with grounding energy. Practice forgiveness and release resentment, as these heavy emotional anchors obstruct the free flow of Wood energy. By mastering your inner emotional state, you unlock your highest potential.

Fire: Force of Transformation

Your Fire element is the engine of your body, governing the heart, small intestine, and circulatory system. Its associated emotion is joy, but when it is mismanaged, it can erupt into anxiety or excessive excitability.

Recognizing Imbalance: The Signals of Overheating

When Fire energy is imbalanced, your internal system sends clear warnings of overheating or chaos.

Physically, this can manifest as heart palpitations, high blood pressure, or a persistent feeling of restlessness and insomnia.

Emotionally, you may experience intense anxiety and struggle with scattered thoughts and a lack of focus. These aren't just symptoms—they're red flags from your internal command center, indicating that your system is running too hot and risking burnout.

Part 5 | *Chapter 14 : The Elemental Guide to Well-Being*

Fire: Strategic Solutions

To strategically nurture your Fire element and restore its powerful flow, deploy the following:

- **Diet** – Command your internal ecosystem with a diet rich in cooling and calming foods. Incorporate bitter foods like dandelion greens and kale to extinguish excess heat. Ensure optimal hydration with water and herbal teas.

- **Activity** – Your body needs to release excess energy in a controlled manner. Engage in calming, rhythmic activities like meditation, walking, and swimming. These practices are a strategic way to settle the mind and body. Avoid over-scheduling to prevent mental and physical burnout, which can lead to a chaotic energy state.

- **Lifestyle** – The most powerful remedy is to manage your internal emotional landscape. Cultivate practices that promote inner peace. Disengage from constant stimulation and social media to reduce anxiety. By consciously creating a calm internal environment, you transform anxiety into a state of focused, vital energy.

Earth: Essence of Stability

Your Earth element is the foundation of your well-being, governing the spleen, stomach, and digestive system. Its associated emotion is worry, but when harnessed effectively, it becomes the ultimate source of thoughtfulness and groundedness.

Recognizing Imbalance: The Signals of Instability

When Earth energy is imbalanced, your system sends clear warnings of stagnation and a lack of foundation.

Physically, this manifests as digestive issues like bloating and indigestion, persistent fatigue, or unexplained weight fluctuations.

Emotionally, you may feel excessively worried and prone to overthinking, lacking a sense of grounding. These are not just symptoms; they are red flags from your internal command center, indicating a break in your fundamental stability.

Part 5 | *Chapter 14 : The Elemental Guide to Well-Being*

Earth: Strategic Solutions

To strategically nurture your Earth element and restore its powerful flow, deploy the following:

- **Diet** – Command your internal ecosystem with a diet rich in grounding and nurturing ingredients. Focus on root vegetables, warm, cooked meals, and naturally sweet flavors from sources like yams and dates. Excessive cold or raw food can weaken your core energy.

- **Activity** – Your body needs stabilizing movement to reinforce its foundation. Engage in activities like walking, light strength training, and gardening to build stability. Intense cardio can further deplete your core energy.

- **Lifestyle** – The most powerful remedy is to manage your internal emotional landscape. Create a stable, predictable routine. Practice mindfulness and gratitude to manage worry. Focus on building and nurturing your core relationships and community, as this provides an emotional foundation that mirrors the stability of the Earth element.

Metal: Power of Discipline

Your Metal element is the architect of your physical and emotional boundaries, governing the lungs, large intestine, and respiratory system. It is associated with sadness, which, when channeled constructively, becomes the ultimate source of discernment and clarity.

Recognizing Imbalance: The Signals of Rigidity

When Metal energy is imbalanced, your system sends clear warnings of rigidity or a lack of fluidity.

Physically, this imbalance can show up as respiratory issues like allergies or asthma, skin problems, or a weakened immune system.

Emotionally, you might experience depression, excessive sadness, or difficulty maintaining personal boundaries. These are not just symptoms—they are red flags from your internal command center, alerting you that your protective systems are compromised.

Metal: Strategic Solutions

To strategically nurture your Metal element and restore its powerful flow, deploy the following blueprint:

- **Diet** – Command your internal ecosystem with a diet rich in pungent, spicy foods to promote cleansing and circulation. Incorporate garlic, onion, ginger, and pungent vegetables. Avoid heavy, greasy foods that can weigh down the system.
- **Activity** – Your body needs movement to cleanse and release. Engage in rhythmic breathing exercises, tai chi, or boxing to promote a clear and disciplined flow of energy.
- **Lifestyle** – The most powerful remedy is to manage your internal emotional landscape. Practice letting go of the past and emotional burdens. Set clear boundaries in your personal and professional life. Practice deep breathing exercises to cleanse the body and mind, and reinforce your energetic and emotional defenses.

Water: Current of Flow

Your Water element is the fluid command center of your body, governing the kidneys, bladder, and skeletal system. It is associated with fear, which, when channeled constructively, becomes the ultimate source of courage and wisdom.

Recognizing Imbalance: The Signals of Depletion

When Water energy is imbalanced, your system sends clear warnings of depletion or overwhelm.

Physically, this can manifest as lower back pain, persistent fatigue, or hormonal imbalances.

Emotionally, you may feel gripped by fear, anxiety, or a profound lack of confidence and willpower. These aren't just symptoms—they are urgent signs from your internal command center, warning of a severe drain on your body's core reserves.

Part 5 | *Chapter 14 : The Elemental Guide to Well-Being*

Water: Strategic Solutions

To strategically nurture your Water element and restore its powerful flow, deploy the following:

- **Diet** – Command your internal ecosystem with a diet rich in hydrating and nourishing foods. Focus on salty foods (in moderation) like seafood, bone broth, and mineral-rich soups. Ensure proper hydration with water throughout the day.

- **Activity** – Your body needs rest and deep restoration to replenish its core energy. Engage in restorative, low-impact activities like yin yoga, gentle swimming, or napping. Avoid overexertion and pushing your body to its limits, as this can deplete your core reserves and lead to physical burnout.

- **Lifestyle** – The most powerful remedy is to manage your internal emotional landscape. Confront your fears and anxieties with a sense of courage and a clear mind. Practice meditation and visualization to cultivate a sense of inner peace and resilience, transforming fear into a wellspring of profound wisdom.

Chapter 15
Elemental Well-Being in Action – Case Studies

The strategy has been defined. Now it's time to see it in action. The following case studies stand as a testament to the transformative power of the health blueprint, revealing how individuals harnessed elemental wisdom to reach and sustain peak performance.

Here, we move beyond theory into real-world application, providing tangible proof that mastering your internal ecosystem isn't just beneficial—it's your ultimate competitive advantage.

Part 5 | *Chapter 15 : Elemental Well-Being in Action – Case Studies*

Case Study: Marcus, Battling Chronic Migraines

Profile and Conflict

Marcus is a top-tier M&A executive whose chart is dominated by the Wood element—the driving force behind his relentless ambition and sharp decisiveness. While professionally successful, he battles debilitating migraines and episodes of uncontrollable anger. His body is physically and emotionally locked in a state of tension—a clear sign that his system is under immense pressure.

The BaZi Diagnosis

Marcus's chart reveals a strong but stagnant Wood element. His innate drive has become an internal burden. The liver, governed by Wood, is in distress, unable to flow freely.

The Strategic Insight

His excess Wood needed a creative outlet. To achieve balance, Marcus needed to find ways to "burn off" his excess energy through Fire-like activities.

The Blueprint for Recovery

- **Release valve** – He began a daily twenty-minute yoga practice to promote heat and dynamic flow, serving as a constructive, Fire-like outlet for his aggression.

- **Emotional expression** – He started to practice journaling and vocalizing his frustrations in a controlled setting, rather than bottling them up. This act of emotional expression is a direct Fire-like action that transforms raw energy into clarity.

- **The outcome** – Marcus's migraines subsided, and the tension that once gripped his body began to ease. By strategically releasing his excess energy, he transformed his anger into a potent, focused ambition. This shift not only helped in achieve professional excellence, it also brought him internal peace.

Part 5 | *Chapter 15 : Elemental Well-Being in Action – Case Studies*

Case Study: Finn, Dealing with Exhaustion

Profile and Conflict

Finn is a brilliant but struggling team leader at McDonald's with a deficient Wood element in his chart. He feels indecisive and overwhelmed by the needs of his team. His lack of drive and vision has led to professional stagnation, and he often feels physically exhausted and mentally drained, unable to find the assertiveness to move forward.

The BaZi Diagnosis

Finn's chart reveals a weak Wood element, reflected in his lack of ambition and decisiveness. This deficiency leaves him vulnerable to external pressures and unable to initiate meaningful change.

The Strategic Insight

Finn's deficient Wood energy needed nurturing. He needed to introduce Water-like activities that would replenish his core energy and restore his courage and willpower.

The Blueprint for Recovery

- **Deep replenishment** – Finn began a restorative practice of yin yoga and meditation, which are deeply nourishing Water-like activities that help build core energy and resilience.

- **Finding wisdom** – He started reading books on strategy and leadership—Water-like activities that cultivate wisdom and clarity. These practices helped replenish his core energy and made him more confident and decisive.

- **The outcome** – Finn found a renewed sense of purpose and drive. By strategically nurturing his core energy, he transformed his indecision into a clear vision and his exhaustion into a powerful ambition.

Part 5 | *Chapter 15 : Elemental Well-Being in Action – Case Studies*

Case Study: Jonathan, Struggling with Emotional Imbalance

Profile and Conflict

Jonathan is a brilliant but struggling entrepreneur whose chart reveals a deficient Fire element. Despite his powerful mind and strong sense of purpose, he struggles from chronic fatigue, a lack of passion, and a deep sense of emotional emptiness. He feels overwhelmed by the complexity of life and struggles to find the motivation to move forward.

The BaZi Diagnosis

Jonathan's chart reveals a weak Fire element. He lacks the foundational energy of joy, passion, and enthusiasm, leaving him vulnerable to apathy and a sense of emotional emptiness.

The Strategic Insight

Jonathan's deficient Fire needed nurturing. Engaging a Wood-like regimen is essential in igniting his inner spark and helping restore structure, ambition, and a clear sense of purpose.

The Blueprint for Recovery

- **Strategic vision** – Jonathan began a daily practice of strategic planning, a Wood-like activity that helps build a sense of purpose and direction.

- **Nourishing growth** – He started to engage in activities that promoted growth and expansion, such as learning a new skill, a Wood-like activity that cultivates a sense of ambition and confidence.

- **The outcome** – By applying the recovery blueprint, Jonathan found a new sense of purpose and resilience. Nurturing his Fire element transformed his apathy into a profound sense of passion and joy, allowing him to command his life with confidence.

Case Study: Sarah, Finding a Solution for Insomnia

Profile and Conflict

Sarah is a charismatic and high-energy tech founder whose chart reveals a strong Fire element, fueling her creativity and enthusiasm. However, her "joy" has tipped into a frantic, anxious energy, leading to chronic insomnia, heart palpitations, and an inability to focus. She is on the edge of burnout.

The BaZi Diagnosis

Sarah's chart indicates an overactive and uncontained Fire element. Her powerful drive for innovation has caused her internal system to overheat, and her frantic energy has depleted her core reserves.

The Strategic Insight

Her chaotic Fire needed to be governed by a controlling force. Sarah needed to introduce Water-like disciplines that would cool and regulate her internal system.

The Blueprint for Recovery

- **Strategic stillness** – Sarah replaced her high-intensity workouts with meditation and yin yoga—low-energy, introspective practices that have a calming, Water-like effect on her nervous system.

- **Restoration and fluidity** – She adopted a diet rich in cooling ingredients and incorporated swimming into her routine—a deeply restorative Water-like activity that soothed both body and mind.

- **The outcome** – Sarah's sleep quality dramatically improved, and her once-scattered mind became sharp and clear. In the process, she learned that true power comes not from constant intensity, but from a strategic balance of high-intensity work and restorative stillness.

Case Study: Carlos, Grappling with Chronic Fatigue

Profile and Conflict

Carlos is a trusted project manager whose chart is dominated by the Earth element—making him an unwavering support system for those around him. He suffers from chronic fatigue, digestive issues, and an overwhelming sense of worry from taking on the emotional burdens of his community.

The BaZi Diagnosis

Carlos's chart reveals a stagnant and overburdened Earth element. His powerful capacity to absorb and process has reached a tipping point, leading to internal congestion and exhaustion.

The Strategic Insight

Carlos's stagnant Earth energy needed a way to process and release its burdens. Performing Metal-like endeavors are essential in providing Carlos with structure and a means to let go of his anxieties.

The Blueprint for Recovery

- **Strategic boundaries** – Through coaching, Carlos learned to manage his tendency to over worry by practicing thought-stopping techniques that helped him create clear boundaries for his mental energy.

- **Active release** – Incorporating light strength training and martial arts into his routine—Metal-like activities that emphasized structure, discipline, and precision—helped him release pent-up energy and made him feel more resilient.

- **The outcome** – Carlos's chronic fatigue and digestive issues significantly improved. By strategically introducing Metal-like disciplines, he transformed his role from a weary caretaker into a resilient leader who could provide sustainable support, starting with himself.

Part 5 | *Chapter 15 : Elemental Well-Being in Action – Case Studies*

Case Study: Claire, Overcoming Overthinking

Profile and Conflict

Claire is a loving and generous person with a deficient Earth element. She constantly gives to others, often at the expense of her own well-being. As a result, she feels completely depleted and overwhelmed by the emotional burdens of those around her. She suffers from persistent overthinking and a deep sense of emotional emptiness.

The Diagnosis

Claire's BaZi Chart shows a deficient Earth element. She lacks the foundational energy of stability and nurturing, making her unable to set boundaries and vulnerable to emotional intrusion.

The Strategic Insight

Claire's deficient Earth energy needed nurturing. Introducing Fire-like disciplines is essential in providing warmth, joy, and a sense of community into her life.

The Blueprint for Recovery

- **Nourishing connections** – Claire began to engage in activities that brought her joy, such as volunteering, a Fire-like activity that helps build a sense of community and connection.

- **Self-care** – She started a daily practice of self-care, a Fire-like activity that nurtures self-love, joy, and emotional warmth. These intentional acts of kindness restored her confidence and self-worth.

- **The outcome** – Claire found a new sense of purpose and resilience. By strategically nurturing her Earth element, she learned to give from a place of abundance, not depletion, and transformed her overthinking into a profound sense of inner peace.

Case Study: Chad, Facing Respiratory Issues

Profile and Conflict

Chad is a brilliant, opinionated innovator with a chart dominated by a robust Metal element, endowing him with exceptional discernment and leadership. Driven by the need for perfection, he struggles with recurring respiratory issues and an inability to be emotionally vulnerable, leading to a guarded and sad demeanor.

The BaZi Diagnosis

Chad's chart reveals an excessive and rigid Metal element. His disciplined nature has created emotional barriers, preventing him from releasing vulnerability or sadness. The lungs—governed by Metal—are compromised, unable to process and release toxins, both physical and emotional.

The Strategic Insight

His rigid Metal energy needed a pathway for release. Making Water-like pursuits necessary to facilitate a fluid movement and emotional expression.

The Blueprint for Recovery

- **Vulnerability practice** – Chad began a journaling practice to acknowledge his deeper emotions, particularly sadness, which he had long suppressed. This Water-like act of introspection helped him release his rigid emotional state.
- **Fluid movement** – He incorporated tai chi, a Water-like movement that promotes fluidity, helping to release physical and emotional rigidity.
- **The outcome** – Chad's respiratory symptoms improved, and he found a greater sense of emotional freedom. By consciously choosing vulnerability, he transformed his guardedness into genuine connection, discovering that true strength lay not in building walls, but in the courage to let them down.

Part 5 | Chapter 15 : Elemental Well-Being in Action – Case Studies

Case Study: Elvie, Tearing Down Emotional Walls

Profile and Conflict

Elvie is a highly successful executive with a weak Metal element in her chart. She prides herself on her ability to lead with honor and structure, but she struggles with setting healthy boundaries and feels constantly overwhelmed by the needs of others. She often feels a deep sadness that she can't express, and she finds it difficult to connect with others on a deeper level.

The BaZi Diagnosis

Elvie's chart indicates a deficient Metal element. She lacks the foundational energy of discipline and boundaries, leaving her vulnerable to emotional intrusion and making her unable to create a clear separation between her work and personal life.

The Strategic Insight

Elvie's deficient Metal needed nurturing. Introducing Earth-like activities to her routine would provide a stable, nourishing foundation and help her build a clear sense of self-worth and boundaries.

The Blueprint for Recovery

- **Grounded nurturing** – Elvie adopted a diet of warm, cooked meals and root vegetables—Earth-like foods that provide a stable, nourishing foundation.

- **Building a foundation** – She started a daily practice of mindfulness and gratitude, Earth-like activities that foster grounding, emotional stability, and self-worth.

- **The outcome** – Elvie found a new sense of clarity and resilience. By strategically nurturing her Metal element, she learned to set healthy boundaries, which allowed her to connect with others on a deeper level and instilled a profound sense of inner peace.

Case Study: Michael, Overcoming Anxiety

Profile and Conflict

Michael is a brilliant but struggling strategist with a deficient Water element. He possesses a deep intuition and a powerful mind, yet he is constantly plagued by anxiety, fear, and a lack of willpower. The complexity of life seems overwhelming, and he struggles to find the inner peace and resilience to navigate it.

The BaZi Diagnosis

Michael's chart indicates a deficient Water element, leaving him without the foundational energies of wisdom and courage, which makes him vulnerable to fear and unable to trust his own intuition.

The Strategic Insight

Michael's weak Water needed intentional nurturing. Practicing Metal-like disciplines is essential in providing structure and a sense of resilience.

The Blueprint for Recovery

- **Fluid discipline** – Michael began a daily meditation practice and tai chi, Metal-like activities that provide structure and a sense of calm.

- **Strategic visualization** – He started a daily practice of visualization, mentally preparing for challenges and envisioning a positive outcome. This Metal-like activity helped him build inner strength and confidence.

- **The outcome** – Michael's anxiety began to subside, and he found a renewed sense of inner peace. By strategically nurturing his Water element, he transformed his fear into wisdom and uncertainty into courage, allowing him to command his life with confidence.

Case Study: Helen, Dealing with Hormonal Imbalance

Profile and Conflict

Helen is an intuitive and creative consultant whose chart is dominated by the Water element, giving her deep emotional sensitivity and the ability to empathize. However, her empathy has become overwhelming, leaving her with a constant sense of dread and resulting in hormonal imbalances and chronic anxiety.

The BaZi Diagnosis

Helen's chart shows an excessive and uncontained Water element. Her deep emotional sensitivity has become a burden, causing her to absorb the worries of others and compromise her core energetic systems.

The Strategic Insight

Helen's strong and overpowering Water element needed a way to release its burden. Incorporating Wood-like endeavors are necessary in fostering an outlet to channel her excessive empathy.

The Blueprint for Recovery

- **Nourishing growth** – She engaged in activities that promoted growth and expansion, such as gardening, a Wood-like activity that channels her nurturing energy into a productive and contained form.

- **Emotional boundaries** – She learned to set firm boundaries, a Wood-like discipline that created a clear structure, allowing her to process her emotions without being overwhelmed by the burdens of others.

- **The outcome** – Helen's anxiety and hormonal imbalances significantly reduced. She learned to harness her profound empathy as a strength, not a burden, and found a renewed sense of purpose by creating a healthy, contained outlet for her emotional energy.

Part 5 | *Chapter 15 : Elemental Well-Being in Action – Case Studies*

Commanding Your Well-Being: A New Strategic Framework

You now possess the definitive framework for understanding the intricate connection between your personal chart and your health. These case studies are a testament to the fact that well-being is not a matter of chance but a strategic equation to be solved. You have learned to identify the distinct needs of both excess and deficient elements within your system, and you have the precise tools to restore harmony.

While BaZi is a complex system with many layers, mastering the principles of excess and deficiency is the most powerful and immediate way to identify potential health issues and command your vitality. This foundational understanding is more than enough to help you build a resilient and balanced life.

Your body is your most valuable asset. It's time to manage it with the same purpose and precision you apply to your life's greatest ambitions. The power to command your well-being is now in your hands.

Part 5 | *Chapter 16 : Finding Your Center: A Gentle Guide to Emotional Well-being*

Chapter 16

Finding Your Center: A Gentle Guide to Emotional Well-being

Your peace is not a luxury—it's the foundation of your power. While the world can feel demanding and chaotic, true strength comes from an inner calm that can't be disturbed. This chapter is your guide to nurturing that inner sanctuary. By understanding the unique ways your energy responds to pressure, you can move beyond simple reactions and create a gentle, loving strategy for your health that preserves your most valuable resource: your capacity for enduring peace.

In this section, we will explore the unique emotional signatures of each of the Ten Profiles, offering a guide to help you recognize your feelings and turn your most vulnerable moments into your greatest source of peace.

Part 5 | *Chapter 16 : Finding Your Center: A Gentle Guide to Emotional Well-being*

A Calm Oasis: Five Simple Acts for Immediate Peace

When the world feels overwhelming, you need a gentle escape.

These five simple acts are a quiet retreat you can find at any moment. They are not grand gestures, but small, kind acts of self-care that can instantly bring you back to a state of calm.

- **The 60-Second Pause** – Stop what you're doing. Find a quiet spot, stand with a gentle, relaxed posture, and rest a hand on your heart. Take three slow, comforting breaths, inhaling for five seconds and exhaling for five. This simple act of presence breaks the cycle of anxiety and brings you back to the quiet of this very moment.

- **The Gentle Unload** – When your mind is a tangled mess of thoughts, find a piece of paper and simply write them all down. Don't worry about grammar or order. Just let the words flow. This simple act of releasing them from your mind and onto the page creates space for clarity and calm.

- **The Body's Release** – Gently stretch your body. Roll your shoulders, bend your neck, or simply shake out your arms and legs. This physical movement releases built-up tension and reminds your body that it is safe to relax.

- **The Sensory Embrace** – Find a simple object nearby and hold it in your hand. Feel its texture, notice its weight, and trace its lines with your fingers. By gently focusing your attention on this simple sensation, you bring your mind back to a peaceful and tangible reality.

- **The Quiet Reflection** – Close your eyes and recall a single moment of genuine peace or joy. It could be a warm cup of tea, a walk in nature, or a happy memory with a loved one. By recalling a moment of comfort, you remind yourself that peace is always within reach.

Direct Resource (DR) Profile

The Emotional Trigger

The Direct Resource's mind finds comfort in order and a clear plan. When a project becomes chaotic or they are forced to make a decision with incomplete information, their sense of safety disappears. This lack of a clear path creates a deep anxiety that feels like being lost in a dense fog.

The Inner Monologue

"This feels so wrong. I can't move forward until I have all the details. What if I make the wrong choice? I can't trust the process if there isn't one." This inner turmoil leads to overthinking and a feeling of being trapped.

The Mindful Reframe

The key isn't to find the perfect plan but to find peace in the imperfection. The Direct Resource Profile can practice the gentle act of "mental minimalism"—focusing only on the single next step that feels clear and within their control. This small act of order reestablishes a sense of calm.

Direct Resource (DR) Profile: The Strategic Action

Instead of trying to perfect the entire project, they can create a simple, small-scale blueprint for the next 24 hours. By building a clear process for just one day, they turn their anxiety into a tool for focused action. They are no longer fighting chaos. They are creating their own stable ground.

The Inner Fortress

The Direct Resource Profile finds their strength by cultivating inner predictability. Their soothing mental practice is to consistently engage in structured breathing. By focusing on the gentle rhythm of the breath—a simple process that is always within their control—they train their mind to find stability from within, regardless of external chaos. This exercise is a psychological anchor.

Indirect Resource (IR) Profile

The Emotional Trigger

The Indirect Resource's spirit is fueled by curiosity and creative insight. When they are stuck in a predictable routine or a system that offers no room for new ideas, their energy stagnates. The lack of intellectual challenge creates a deep restlessness and suffocation, leading to a physical and mental fatigue that feels like boredom.

The Inner Monologue

"This isn't inspiring. I'm just going through the motions. There has to be a better way, a different approach, but I can't think of anything. I feel trapped and uninspired." This inner battle leads to lethargy and a feeling of being mentally drained.

The Mindful Reframe

The key is not to find the next great idea but to give your mind the freedom to wander. The Indirect Resource Profile can practice intuitive play—deliberately allowing their thoughts to explore new, unrelated topics without judgment. This releases the pressure to perform and reopens the flow of creative energy.

Indirect Resource (IR) Profile: The Strategic Action

They can schedule a "strategic day" once a month, where they step away from all routine tasks. By dedicating time to exploring new art, books, or environments, they are not just relaxing; they are actively refilling their creative well. This intentional act of exploration becomes a powerful source of future innovation.

The Inner Fortress

The Indirect Resource Profile finds their strength by cultivating intellectual freedom. Their soothing mental practice is to consistently engage in "pattern disruption." By intentionally breaking a small, routine habit each day—like taking a new route to work or eating in a different order—they train their mind to seek out and create new pathways, preparing it to find unique solutions in times of chaos.

Part 5 | *Chapter 16 : Finding Your Center: A Gentle Guide to Emotional Well-being*

Friend (F) Profile

The Emotional Trigger

The Friends Profile's strength comes from their community. When they face isolation or feel let down by others, their natural support system is compromised. This creates a profound sense of loneliness and self-doubt, as if they are suddenly standing alone.

The Inner Monologue

"I'm on my own here. I cannot trust anyone. Why didn't they support me? I have to do this all myself." This inner narrative of disconnection erodes their sense of self-worth and purpose.

The Mindful Reframe

The key is to remember that your power is not in your independence, but in your connections. The Friend Profile can practice "anchoring in trust"—consciously reaching out to a single, trusted peer to voice their concerns. This act of vulnerability is a strength, not a weakness.

Friend (F) Profile: The Strategic Action

Instead of trying to solve the problem alone, they can gently reframe the challenge as a collective issue. By transparently bringing the issue to their trusted network, they not only restore their own mental balance but also rally their community. This turns a personal vulnerability into an unshakable bond.

The Inner Fortress

The Friend Profile finds their strength by cultivating emotional connection. Their soothing mental practice is to consistently engage in "network gardening." By spending five minutes each day sending a short, genuine message of appreciation or support to someone in their network, they actively strengthen their safety net and reinforce the psychological truth that they are supported and not alone.

Rob Wealth (RW) Profile

The Emotional Trigger

The Rob Wealth's energy is a passionate drive that needs a purpose. When they lack a clear goal, a friendly rival, or a new challenge, their drive turns inward. This creates a deep restlessness and a tendency toward self-sabotage, as if their inner fire is consuming them from within.

The Inner Monologue

"What's the point? This is too easy. I am bored. I feel restless and agitated. I need a challenge." This mental itch for a new goal can lead to them creating unnecessary conflict or drama just to feel alive.

The Mindful Reframe

The key is to realize that your most valuable competition is with yourself. The Rob Wealth Profile can practice "internalizing the game," by focusing on personal growth and self-mastery instead of an external rival. This redirects their passionate fire into a productive, endless pursuit.

Rob Wealth Profile: The Strategic Action

They thrive by setting their own benchmarks—whether it's learning a new skill, hitting a personal record in a sport, or building something from the ground up. It's not just about winning; it's about transforming the challenge into a journey of growth and reinvention.

The Inner Fortress

The Rob Wealth Profile finds their strength by cultivating personal discipline. Their soothing mental practice is to consistently engage in "micro-competitions." By finding small, personal, nonnegotiable goals each day—like beating their own time in a task or learning one new word—they feed their need for challenge and validation from within, making them less dependent on external validation.

Eating God (EG) Profile

The Emotional Trigger

The Eating God's spirit is tied to their creative flow. When they are forced to conform to rigid rules or a system that stifles personal expression, their energy becomes stagnant. This creates a profound sense of creative emptiness and can lead to a feeling of being trapped.

The Inner Monologue

"This is so boring. I'm just a cog in a machine. My ideas don't matter. I feel numb and uninspired." This inner feeling of being suppressed can lead to creative block and a complete loss of motivation.

The Mindful Reframe

The key is to find freedom within constraint. The Eating God Profile can practice "constraint as a canvas," by accepting the rules as a puzzle to be solved creatively. This shifts their mindset from frustration to focused play.

Eating God (EG) Profile: The Strategic Action

They can intentionally seek out a small, low-stakes creative outlet like sketching, cooking a new meal, or rearranging their workspace. By creating a habit of daily creative expression, they keep their mental flow open and ensure their most valuable ideas are always ready when they are needed.

The Inner Fortress

The Eating God Profile finds their strength by cultivating creative expression. Their soothing mental practice is to consistently engage in sensory discovery. By spending five minutes a day intentionally focusing on a single sensation—the color of a cup, the texture of a stone, the sound of a street—they train their mind to find novelty and beauty in the mundane, ensuring their creative well never runs dry.

Hurting Officer (HO) Profile

The Emotional Trigger

The Hurting Officer's energy is a powerful force for change. When their innovative ideas are met with resistance or ignored, their natural drive to challenge the status quo turns into frustration and resentment. This bottled-up energy creates a physical and mental tension that feels like a weight on their shoulders.

The Inner Monologue

"This is a stupid way of doing things. Why won't they listen to me? I cannot believe how stagnant this is. It's so unfair." This inner outrage becomes a source of stress that can lead to burnout and cynicism.

The Mindful Reframe

The key isn't to fight every battle but to choose the ones that matter. The Hurting Officer Profile can practice "channeling the rebellion," by consciously redirecting their energy from frustration to strategic action. This involves stepping back to analyze the situation from a higher perspective.

Hurting Officer (HO) Profile: The Strategic Action

Instead of trying to convince people who are resistant, they can focus on building a small, undeniable proof of concept. By creating a small-scale, successful change, they don't just solve a problem—they show a new path forward that is impossible to ignore. They become a catalyst for change, not a crusader against resistance.

The Inner Fortress

The Hurting Officer finds their strength by cultivating strategic detachment. Their soothing mental practice is to consistently engage in "intellectual inventory." By spending time each day dispassionately documenting every flaw they see and every potential solution without trying to implement them, they channel their rebellious energy into a structured, analytical exercise that prevents it from turning into a destructive force.

Direct Wealth (DW) Profile

The Emotional Trigger

The Direct Wealth Profile's mental health is tied to a sense of predictability and financial stability. When they face a sudden loss of control or financial unpredictability, their foundational sense of security is compromised. This creates a deep-seated anxiety and a feeling of powerlessness.

The Inner Monologue

"I can't control this. What if I lose everything? This is a disaster. I feel like I'm not in command." This internal fear leads to overthinking and a panicked desire to regain control, which can lead to rash decisions.

The Mindful Reframe

The key isn't to control every outcome but to trust in your ability to create value. The Direct Wealth Profile can practice "resilience through ritual," by focusing on a single, non-financial routine they can fully control, like a daily workout or meditation. This simple act of creating order in one area of life reminds them that their power is internal, not external.

Direct Wealth (DW) Profile: The Strategic Action

Instead of chasing every market signal, they can create a "scenario playbook" that outlines their response to various downturns. By transforming a feared scenario into a plan, they move from a state of reactive fear to one of strategic preparedness. They don't just manage risk; they use their anxiety to get ahead of it.

The Inner Fortress

The Direct Wealth Profile finds their strength by cultivating a sense of abundance. Their soothing mental practice is to consistently engage in "value mapping." By spending a few minutes each day listing three non-monetary assets they created or received—a valuable connection, a new piece of knowledge, a moment of joy—they train their mind to recognize that their wealth is not limited to their bank account.

Indirect Wealth (IW) Profile

The Emotional Trigger

The Indirect Wealth Profile's mind is a kaleidoscope of intuitive insights. When they are forced to conform to a rigid structure or a conventional path, their intuition feels stifled. This lack of creative freedom creates a profound restlessness and a deep sense of being trapped.

The Inner Monologue

"I hate this. This isn't how it's supposed to be. I see a different way, but I can't explain it. I feel like I'm being forced to hide my true self." This inner conflict between their intuition and the external world creates a feeling of being inauthentic and disengaged.

The Mindful Reframe

The key is to find freedom in every moment. The Indirect Wealth Profile can practice "intellectual exploration," by deliberately allowing their mind to wander and explore completely unrelated topics. This act of mental rebellion reclaims their intuitive power and reminds them that their greatest insights come from breaking the rules.

Part 5 | *Chapter 16 : Finding Your Center: A Gentle Guide to Emotional Well-being*

Indirect Wealth (IW) Profile: The Strategic Action

They can seek out small, unconventional opportunities to test their intuition. This could be a small investment in a high-risk company, or a low-stakes side project. By allowing themselves to take small, intuitive bets, they sharpen their gut instincts and turn their restlessness into a tool for innovation.

The Inner Fortress

The Indirect Wealth Profile finds their strength by cultivating cognitive agility. Their soothing mental practice is to consistently engage in "mental prototyping." By taking a simple, everyday problem and spending five minutes imagining ten completely different, non-conventional ways to solve it, they train their mind to embrace complexity and find a path forward where others see only a dead end.

Direct Officer (DO) Profile

The Emotional Trigger

The Direct Officer Profile's sense of self is tied to a need for order, justice, and accountability. When they face a situation of profound injustice, a breach of integrity, or a lack of accountability, their inner sense of fairness is violated. This creates intense frustration and a physical tension that feels like a weight on their shoulders.

The Inner Monologue

"This isn't right. This is unfair. How can I let this stand? I must take action." This inner voice of righteousness can become a source of stress, leading to a constant state of combativeness and burnout.

The Mindful Reframe

The key isn't to fight every battle but to uphold the system itself. The Direct Officer Profile can practice "upholding the principle, not the person." By focusing on a clear, just process, they can detach from the emotional weight of individual conflict and ensure that the system itself maintains order.

Direct Officer Profile: The Strategic Action

Instead of engaging in a personal conflict, they can create a clear, documented code of conduct. By enforcing the rules of the system, they don't just solve the problem; they create an entire culture of integrity. This frees their mental energy from the emotional burden of injustice and allows them to lead with calm, unwavering authority.

The Inner Fortress

The Direct Officer Profile finds their strength by cultivating moral clarity. Their soothing mental practice is to consistently engage in "ethical journaling." By spending a few minutes each day reflecting on a decision and how it aligns with their core values, they build a powerful internal compass that guides them through conflict and reduces the mental burden of ethical dilemmas.

Part 5 | *Chapter 16 : Finding Your Center: A Gentle Guide to Emotional Well-being*

Seven Killings Profile

The Emotional Trigger

The Seven Killings's energy is a powerful engine of discipline and resolve. When they are not facing a clear, high-stakes challenge, their drive turns inward. This lack of external pressure creates a profound restlessness and anxiety, as if they are a warrior without a battle.

The Inner Monologue

"I feel restless. This is too easy. I need a challenge; I need to be in control of something. I'm losing my edge." This inner battle can lead them to create unnecessary conflict or to take on extreme challenges just to feel alive.

The Mindful Reframe

The key isn't to find the next great battle but to realize that your ultimate rival is yourself. The Seven Killings Profile can practice self-mastery, by focusing their relentless drive on personal growth and discipline. This redirects their warrior's spirit into an endless and productive pursuit.

Seven Killings (7K) Profile: The Strategic Action

They can create a new, personal competition with a clear metric. This could be mastering a new skill, setting a new personal best in a sport, or taking on a new creative project. By constantly challenging themselves, they don't just win the game; they evolve it.

The Inner Fortress

The Seven Killings finds their strength by cultivating focused discipline. Their soothing mental practice is to consistently engage in "one-task mastery." By spending fifteen minutes each day doing a single, nonnegotiable task with perfect focus, they train their mind to find purpose in any situation, no matter how small, building an unshakable sense of accomplishment and control.

Chapter 17
Finding Your Center in Action – Case Studies

Understanding your energetic profile is a powerful act of self-discovery, but true mastery is found in practice. In the previous chapter, we explored the emotional signals of each profile. Now, we will bring those insights to life through ten true-to-life scenarios.

This chapter is a collection of happy-ever-after stories. They are not about finding a perfect life but about what happens when you find your true north and use your "free will" to turn life's most challenging moments into your greatest victories.

Each story is a living testament to a simple, profound truth: Life is what we are given, and with awareness, we can create something beautiful with it.

An amazing life is not something you are simply handed, but something you build—an act of quiet courage that begins with a healthy mind.

Case Study: Arvin, Direct Resource (DR) Profile

Arvin, a meticulous project manager for a small business, felt his anxiety spike every time his carefully planned weekend fell apart. When his partner impulsively suggested a last-minute road trip, Arvin's mind immediately raced to every possible problem: traffic, no hotel reservations, and no planned activities. Arvin's inner world, designed for peace, became a prison of what-ifs.

The BaZi Diagnosis

Arvin's chart revealed a core need for stability and a natural talent for building solid foundations. His greatest strength—the ability to plan—had become a weakness, making him deeply vulnerable to the anxiety of the unplanned. His sense of well-being was mistakenly tied to external control, not internal calm.

The BaZi reading was Arvin's moment of clarity. He realized he could not control the world, but he could control his internal response. Arvin shifted his focus from building an external itinerary to building an internal one. Before any unplanned event, Arvin would now take five minutes to focus on what he could control: packing a small bag of comforting items like a favorite book and his noise-canceling headphones.

The Transformation

By cultivating an unshakable internal oasis of calm, Arvin found his joy was no longer dependent on a flawless plan. He is now able to relax and enjoy the moment, learning that the best parts of any adventure are often the ones you never saw coming.

Case Study: Olivia, Indirect Resource (IR) Profile

Olivia, a passionate amateur painter, spent her evenings in her studio, lost in a world of color and form. But she felt a deep sense of loneliness because her family just didn't "get it." Her mother would ask, "What are you even going to do with all those paintings?" Making Olivia feel like her most vital emotional outlet was just a waste of time. She loved them, but she felt profoundly misunderstood.

The BaZi Diagnosis

Olivia's chart revealed a soul that thrives on introspection and creative expression. Her happiness was tied to nurturing her rich inner world. The judgment from others wasn't an attack on her hobby—it was a symptom of a fundamental misalignment between her inner world and the outer one. Her need to be "useful" in the eyes of others was suffocating her creative spirit.

The BaZi reading was a powerful act of validation. Olivia realized her art wasn't for anyone else—it was for her. It was her way of processing emotions and finding inner peace. She set new boundaries. She stopped seeking external validation and, instead, protected her creative time. When someone questioned her art, she would simply smile and say, "It's for me. It makes me happy."

The Transformation

Olivia's inner world flourished. She found a community of artists who understood her, and the joy of her painting became so palpable that her family, seeing her quiet contentment, eventually stopped asking questions. She learned that emotional wellness is not found in being understood by everyone, but in being true to yourself.

Case Study: Ace, Friend (F) Profile

Ace was a community leader and a master of friendship. He organized birthday dinners, coached his kid's soccer team, and was the first person his friends called in a crisis. But his social calendar was a cage. He constantly felt overwhelmed and stretched thin, running from one commitment to the next. He couldn't say no, convinced that his self-worth was directly tied to how much he gave to others. His deep desire for connection had turned into a relentless cycle of burnout.

The BaZi Diagnosis

Ace's chart showed a natural gift for building community and a deep-seated need for connection. However, his profile's imbalance meant his friendships were a one-way street, where he gave and others received. His need for belonging was so strong that he had let his boundaries crumble, turning his community into a source of exhaustion, not support.

Ace's BaZi reading was a wake-up call. He learned that true friendship is a two-way street, and his worth was not in his output, but in his ability to be present. He began a powerful practice of a strategic no. He started to protect his time, gently declining invitations he knew would drain him. He also began to use his gift for connection to ask for help when he needed it.

The Transformation

By setting firm boundaries, Ace found his friendships became more meaningful and less exhausting. He learned that saying no to one thing allowed him to be fully present for the things that truly mattered. He stopped being the "friend" everyone called and became a deeply loved member of his community, both giving and receiving.

Part 5 | *Chapter 17 : Finding Your Center in Action – Case Studies*

Case Study: Carla, Rob Wealth (RW) Profile

Carla was trapped in a relentless game of comparison. She was a marketing manager who was always looking at what her colleagues were doing. At home, she constantly felt the need to post a more curated, enviable life on social media. She would throw elaborate dinner parties and go on expensive vacations, not for her own joy, but to outshine her friends. This constant need to win left her feeling deeply lonely and insecure.

The BaZi Diagnosis

Carla's chart revealed a natural inclination for competition and a powerful drive to stand out. Her greatest strength—her ambition—had become a source of misery, as she was constantly comparing herself to others. She had lost her true north, allowing external comparisons to dictate her life's direction.

The BaZi reading brought a moment of profound insight. Carla realized that the only person she should be competing with was herself. She started a new, radical practice. She stopped curating her life for others and started living it for herself. She took a step back from social media, focusing on simple joys like cooking a meal she loved or going for a walk, without the need to document it for the world to see.

The Transformation

By detaching from the comparison game, Carla found her self-worth was no longer a moving target. She discovered a deep sense of peace in being enough, exactly as she was. Her greatest victory was not in outshining others but in reclaiming her own joy.

Part 5 | *Chapter 17 : Finding Your Center in Action – Case Studies*

Case Study: Irish, Eating God (EG) Profile

Irish, a stay-at-home mother of two, had dedicated her life to her family. She was a master baker, a creative homemaker, and the emotional rock for everyone in her home. But beneath the surface, she felt a profound sense of emptiness. She had lost herself in the act of giving, with no creative outlet for her own passions. The joy she once found in her hobbies had vanished, replaced by a quiet sense of unfulfillment.

The BaZi Diagnosis

Irish's chart revealed a creative, nurturing soul who finds joy in expression. Her energy was that of a giver, but she had been giving everything to others and nothing to herself. The chart showed her that her emotional well-being was tied to her ability to create, and she had allowed a lack of a creative outlet to starve her soul.

The BaZi reading was a powerful validation of her feelings. Irish realized her purpose was not just to nurture others, but to nurture her own creative spirit. She made a bold choice: She carved out two hours a week to return to painting. She did not seek to sell anything or become famous; she just painted for the pure joy of it.

The Transformation

As she made space for her creativity, Irish's entire emotional landscape shifted. Her joy became infectious, and she felt a sense of purpose beyond her family. She learned that a truly full life is not one where you give endlessly, but one where you also create and receive.

Case Study: Jessie, Hurting Officer (HO) Profile

Jessie—a sales director known for his razor-sharp wit and unfiltered honesty—was the person everyone approached for the unvarnished truth. But his frankness often hurt those he loved. His wife would share a problem, and he would immediately offer a cold, "logical" solution, leaving her feeling hurt and dismissed. He could not understand why his practical, well-meaning advice was so often met with tears.

The BaZi Diagnosis

Jessie's Hurting Officer chart revealed a genius for seeing flaws and improving systems. This was his strength—but also his greatest liability. He was subconsciously applying his professional mind to his personal life, not realizing that what his wife needed was empathy, not a solution. His love was filtered through logic, making it difficult to receive.

The BaZi reading exposed the flaw in his operating system. Jessie realized his honesty was a weapon, not a tool, when used without emotional awareness. He started to practice a new form of empathy. When his wife came to him with a problem, he made a conscious choice to not offer a solution. Instead, he would simply say, "That sounds hard. Tell me more."

The Transformation

The silence and unspoken friction in their relationship began to dissolve. He learned that his greatest strength was not in his ability to fix problems, but in his ability to provide a safe space where his partner could simply be heard.

Case Study: Chris, Direct Wealth (DW) Profile

Chris, a dedicated accountant, showed his love through practical acts. He paid the bills on time, managed the family budget, and made sure the car was always serviced. But he felt a deep sense of resentment that his partner seemed to take it all for granted. He longed for spontaneous expressions of affection, but he didn't know how to ask for them. He felt like a steady foundation that was never truly appreciated for the emotional security it provided.

The BaZi Diagnosis

Chris's Direct Wealth chart revealed a core nature of stability and practicality. The chart exposed his profound weakness: He expected others to intuitively understand his emotional needs, and his own desire for spontaneity was being stifled by his unwavering commitment to routine.

The BaZi reading was a breakthrough for Chris. He realized that his partner couldn't read his mind, and that his love for her was an active, emotional choice. He made a transformative change. He began to practice speaking his emotional needs out loud, saying things like, "I would love a hug right now," or "Could we take an hour to just hang out?" He also planned a weekly "spontaneity hour" where he would surprise his partner with an impromptu date or an unexpected treat.

The Transformation

Chris's quiet resentment was replaced by a sense of being truly seen and loved. He learned that an amazing life is not built on predictable routine, but on the courage to express your needs.

Case Study: Jessica, Indirect Wealth (IW) Profile

Jessica, a talented freelance graphic designer, had a new, exciting idea every six months. She'd launch a new project, teach herself a new skill, or join a new social club. But her ventures never stuck, and she felt a deep sense of shame and instability. Her boyfriend, a homebody, struggled to keep up with her constant need for new experiences, which made her feel emotionally caged. She was a high-stakes player in a market of transient passions.

The BaZi Diagnosis

Jessica's chart revealed a natural aptitude for risk and a passion for novelty. She was designed to explore new ideas and monetize risk. The chart exposed her profound weakness: Her constant motion was an avoidance tactic, a fear of committing to one thing—or one person—and missing out on the next adventure. Her pursuit of newness was a source of great stress.

The BaZi reading helped Jessica understand that a long-term relationship was the ultimate high-value asset, not a cage. She channeled her adventurous energy into building a shared future. She learned to view her relationship not as a stable port, but as a new and exciting journey they could embark on together. She began to use her creative energy to design joint projects with her partner, like building a garden or renovating a room.

The Transformation

Jessica's fear of missing out was replaced by a powerful motivation to build something lasting. She learned that the greatest adventure wasn't in fleeting opportunities, but in forging a lasting union of love and joint ambition.

Case Study: Darren, Direct Officer (DO) Profile

Darren was a manager at a large retail store, and his perfectionism and need for control bled into his personal life. He would micromanage his partner's packing for a weekend trip, making sure every item was perfectly organized. His love, though expressed through acts of duty and responsibility, felt more like a command than a gift. His partner felt constantly judged, and their relationship became a series of battles over minor details.

The BaZi Diagnosis

Darren's Direct Officer chart revealed a natural leader who excels at order and command. His strength, however, had become his greatest weakness. His need for perfection was suffocating those he loved. He showed love by imposing his standards on others, not realizing that his partner needed to feel free, not controlled.

The BaZi reading gave Darren a powerful insight: A leader's true power is not in control, but in building a supportive environment where others can thrive. Darren made a bold choice. He consciously began to decouple his professional standards from his personal life. He would intentionally step back and let his partner handle things her way, even if it wasn't his "perfect" way. He also began a practice of "unconditional appreciation," praising his partner for her effort, not just the outcome.

The Transformation

The constant battles dissolved. Darren learned that his greatest act of love was not in control, but in trust. His partner felt a deep sense of security and love from him, and their relationship shifted from one of pressure to one of profound respect.

Part 5 | *Chapter 17 : Finding Your Center in Action – Case Studies*

Case Study: Rachel, Seven Killings (7K) Profile

Rachel, an athlete, was a fierce protector of her friends and family. When her best friend was heartbroken over a breakup, Rachel's first instinct was to go on the offensive. "You need to block him, delete his number, and get a new dating profile immediately," she'd declare. She was trying to "solve" her friend's pain, not realizing her intense, strategic energy came across as insensitive and judgmental. Her friend just wanted to be heard, but to Rachel, a problem that wasn't being solved felt like a wasted opportunity.

The BaZi Diagnosis

Rachel's chart revealed a powerful, protective energy. Her profile was that of a general, forged in the crucible of conflict. Her greatest strength—her ability to go on the offensive—had become her greatest weakness, as she was instinctively treating emotional pain as a challenge to be solved, not a feeling to be felt.

The BaZi reading was the intelligence report that showed Rachel her battlefield mentality was alienating the people she loved most. She learned her greatest act of protection wasn't guarding against external threats, but in creating an emotional sanctuary—a space where others could simply be. She began a powerful practice of listening. She consciously quieted the "battlefield" in her mind and just said, "I'm here for you."

The Transformation

The friction in her friendships was replaced by a shared peace. Rachel learned her greatest act of love was not in fixing someone's problems, but in providing a safe space where they could simply be vulnerable. Her relationships deepened into a profound intimacy she had never experienced before.

Part 6
Move with Clarity

You have successfully completed the strategic blueprints for your wealth, relationships, and health. You have mastered the foundational pillars of a truly aligned life.

This final part is not a conclusion—it is your ultimate instruction manual for commanding your legacy.

It is about integrating all your mastery to make the ultimate investment of all: the investment in yourself. It ensures that you have the strategic endurance and profound clarity to lead your life with purpose, from this moment forward.

Chapter 18
Your Transformation Awaits: The Ripple Effect of Mastery

You've now embarked on an incredible journey into the heart of your BaZi Destiny Blueprint. This book isn't just about providing information—it's about empowering you with profound insights that spark real, positive changes in your life.

By understanding your unique energetic makeup, you are no longer drifting through life's currents. You are learning to read the map, adjust your sails, and steer your ship with confidence and grace. The true value of this wisdom extends far beyond your personal understanding, creating a beautiful ripple effect that elevates not only your own life but also the lives of those around you.

The Unwavering Command of Self

Imagine truly understanding why you are the way you are. This knowledge fosters deep self-acceptance, dissolves self-judgment, and cultivates profound self-love. You embrace your strengths and strategically work with your challenges, knowing they are all part of your unique design. This authentic confidence is magnetic, drawing positive experiences and genuine connections into your life.

Empowered Decision-Making

With BaZi destiny reading, you gain a powerful framework for making choices that align with your authentic self and your energetic flow. No more second-guessing. You can:

- Discover career paths where you'll thrive, aligning with your innate talents and wealth potential.

- Understand your relationship dynamics, attracting harmonious connections and nurturing existing ones with greater empathy and patience, or finding true love.

- Develop personalized strategies for wealth creation and management that resonate with your unique financial blueprint.

- Gain insights into your energetic predisposition, allowing you to proactively care for your well-being and maintain vitality.

Proactive Problem-Solving and Optimized Resilience

Instead of reacting to dilemmas, you become proactive. Your BaZi chart is like a personalized growth roadmap that allows you to anticipate energetic shifts, leverage favorable periods, and navigate challenging times with a calm foresight.

This transforms dilemmas into opportunities for growth, moving you from aimless striving to purposeful development.

Part 6 | *Chapter 18 : Your Transformation Awaits: The Ripple Effect of Mastery*

The Ripple Effect: Commanding Your World

The positive impact of your journey extends outward, transforming your interactions and relationships in profound ways.

When you understand the energetic blueprints of your loved ones, you develop profound empathy, allowing you to tailor your communication style, dissolve conflicts, and create more loving and harmonious relationships with family, friends, and colleagues. You become a beacon of understanding, creating a positive ripple effect that elevates not only your life but also the lives of those you cherish.

This book is more than just pages of information—it's an invitation to step into a life of greater clarity, empowerment, and joy. It's a gentle nudge to embrace your destiny, not as a fixed outcome, but as a vibrant, living blueprint that you can consciously co-create.

Chapter 19
Commanding Your Legacy: The Ultimate Investment in Self

You have completed the first phase of your mastery, journeying into the core of your BaZi Destiny Blueprint. This knowledge is not a static tool—it is a living instrument, ready for your active engagement. The true power of this book is realized not in its pages, but in your deliberate action. This is where you transform a theoretical framework into a living, breathing command of your life.

This book has given you the foundational knowledge to begin your journey of self-command. While the BaZi Destiny Chart is a profound and complex system, the insights you now hold are more than enough to empower you. You now understand that your life is not a matter of chance, but a strategic equation to be solved.

Your Personal Strategic Playbook

This book has equipped you to become the chief strategist of your own well-being. By engaging with this wisdom, you are already building a more profound and purposeful life. Here are the core strategies you can immediately deploy:

- **Practice conscious command** – Your Day Master and Energetic Profile are your primary guides. Before any pivotal decision—in a negotiation, a relationship, or a health choice—pause to consult your blueprint. This conscious approach empowers you to act with greater purpose and alignment, ensuring every move you make is a strategic one.

- **Become an elemental observer** – Begin to read the energetic landscape of your life. Is your workplace driven by aggressive Wood energy? Is your home filled with nurturing Earth? By becoming attuned to the elements around you, you gain an invaluable form of intelligence that informs your every interaction.

- **Implement strategic adjustments** – The health blueprints revealed imbalances and their remedies. Now, you can proactively apply these insights. If you find yourself in a state of overwhelm, strategically introduce the nourishing element your chart needs. This small, consistent action builds a foundation of true grace.

Beyond Personal Mastery: The Strategic Command of Destiny

The BaZi Destiny Chart is a vital, strategic tool that moves you past self-understanding to commanding your most valuable human capital and navigating high-stakes decisions. By first mastering your own energetic code, you gain the profound ability to decode the energies of others.

For every reader:

- For you, who is at a crossroads of your life, grappling with where to focus your energy.
- For you, who is at the beginning of your journey and wants to discover your optimal place and purpose in the world.
- For those seeking to understand and proactively manage their core physical and energetic health.
- For parents seeking an essential instruction manual for their children, and for individuals navigating complex relationships with parents, bosses, and colleagues.

And for everyone seeking to unlock their full, aligned potential, this blueprint is the powerful guide.

For Wealth and Business Strategy:

The BaZi chart provides a decisive strategic advantage in all financial and professional endeavors:

- For entrepreneurs and HR leaders: It allows you to move past resumes to align an individual's core energy with the demands of their role and the team dynamics, proactively mitigating friction and optimizing performance.

- For maximizing human capital, it acts as a decisive tool for talent deployment, ensuring key personnel are placed exactly where they generate maximum value and minimal resistance.

- In business partnerships: It serves as the core due diligence, revealing a partner's fundamental drivers to ensure your collaborative energies are perfectly aligned to accelerate toward shared goals, not clash in conflict.

For Relationships and Connection:

The chart offers the CLARITY to transform all human dynamics:

- In conflicts: It identifies the "bridging element" required to quickly move past friction and secure the desired outcome in high-stakes negotiations or complex family issues.

- In romantic compatibility: It offers essential foresight, a powerful blueprint to know before you emotionally invest, allowing you to forge a bond based on deep, energetic synergy rather than a fleeting connection that leads to an emotional dead end.

For Health and Personal Power:

The profound application of this blueprint ensures your long-term success is sustainable:

- For maximizing long-term power: The chart reveals your specific energetic vulnerabilities, acting as a proactive health diagnostic to ensure your physical vitality can sustain your ambitious professional and personal drives.

This integrated approach means that by mastering the foundational energetic flow of your life—from your relationships to your finances—you achieve a state of equilibrium that prepares you for your next level of strategic development.

Part 6 | *Chapter 19 : Commanding Your Legacy:The Ultimate Investment in Self*

The Next Phase: The Power of Precision and Strategy

Command Your Destiny: The Benefits of a One-on-One BaZi Strategy Session

When you are ready to take your mastery from knowledge to transformative implementation, a deeper, personalized strategy session awaits.

A personalized BaZi strategy session with me is not a forecast—it's a strategic deep dive into your unique energetic blueprint. By moving past the general principles found in this book, we work together in this session to develop the tactics you need to proactively command your life's trajectory.

Here's what a dedicated consultation will strategically solve for you:

- **Strategic CLARITY on the root cause:** Move beyond the guesswork. A personalized session gives you unwavering CLARITY by identifying the exact elemental imbalance in your chart that is causing friction. We then develop customized strategies and coping mechanisms to address the root causes of your challenges and reveal the most direct path to your goals.

- **Unlocking your niche potential (The Money Map):** Your BaZi chart is a treasure map of your unique gifts. A session provides specific industry and role alignment, guiding you away from time-wasting efforts and directly toward the ventures where your specific profile is guaranteed to maximize wealth and influence.

- **Decoding complex relational conflicts:** Gain a profound, solution-based understanding of a key dynamic in your life. We identify the precise energetic clashes and develop specific, targeted communication and coping strategies to dissolve the misunderstanding and transform that relationship into a supportive asset.

- **Proactive health and energy management:** We move beyond vulnerabilities to build a strategic energetic plan. A session empowers you to identify which specific organs and elements are weakest today, providing actionable lifestyle adjustments and coaching techniques to ensure you operate at peak performance and sustain your long-term success.

The Power of Your Personal Timeline: The BaZi Annual Retainer Service (Ongoing Collaboration)

A one-time session provides the foundational blueprint, but when you are ready for ongoing collaboration and taking your mastery to the next level, my annual retainer service is available to you. This service transforms your Destiny Blueprint into a personalized timeline of your energetic flow.

This isn't just about reading the map—it's about navigating it in real time with a strategic partner.

- **Maximize:** You will know precisely when to launch new ventures, make strategic investments, or forge critical partnerships. These are the periods where the universe is aligning with your blueprint, creating a tailwind for your ambitions.

- **Manage:** You will also be prepared to navigate the months that require a more disciplined approach. With this foresight, you can mitigate risks, manage potential conflicts, and preserve your resources, ensuring you move through every cycle with grace.

This is the powerful differentiator of a BaZi Destiny strategy: transforming a static blueprint into an active, strategic command of your life's most critical moments.

Part 6 | *Chapter 19 : Commanding Your Legacy:The Ultimate Investment in Self*

Your Legacy Awaits: Forge Your Destiny

You have mastered the foundational language of your Destiny Blueprint. You now hold the CLARITY to move from merely understanding your potential to actively unleashing it with masterful command.

This book is more than a guide; it is a strategic manual for a life of purpose, designed to be a durable, generational resource. The insights within are your permanent toolkit—a powerful reference you can turn to whenever you face a new crossroads, a complex relationship, or a high-stakes decision.

My greatest hope is that this wisdom serves you profoundly. I encourage you to pass this book along—to your children, to their children, and to anyone you feel is ready to command their destiny. This is the knowledge you can be proud to recommend and share.

You have already done the most critical work by committing to this path. I wish you the very best as you step into the next phase of your journey, moving with purpose, power, grace and Clarity.

Should you ever wish to explore your BaZi Destiny Blueprint with greater depth and precision, you can find further resources, articles, and educational materials on my website: www.eastwestfengshuisolutions.com

May your life be filled with abundant joy and profound CLARITY.

Move with Clarity,

Master Judith McKenzie

www.ingramcontent.com/pod-product-compliance
Lightning Source LLC
Chambersburg PA
CBHW051620010526
44119CB00009B/221